"This is a very accessible, inspiring book for entrepreneurs and managers.
**Walter Kuemmerle, President, Kuemmerle Research Group, Ltd. and fo
Professor, Harvard Business School.**

"Putting the customer at the centre of your company strategy isn't new.
itself. But simply 'knowing' isn't 'doing'. What Paul O'Dea does in this book that is so importa
entrepreneurial teams simple, pragmatic tools to enable them to define, refine, communicate and execute on
that strategy. Teams with high-growth ambitions should read and use this book."
Brian Caulfield, Serial Entrepreneur, VC and Angel Investor

"This book is a great read. It is not just a great read; it brings superb clarity to how to answer the big questions
that must be addressed to be successful in business, whatever stage your business is at. Essential reading at
least once a year for anyone involved in or interested in shaping a company's direction."
Bernie Cullinan, CEO, Clarigen

"Paul's new book, *The Business Battlecard* presents a post credit crunch blueprint for a re-start/think. It encourages
businesses to deeply question, take stock, align & re-energise. It amplifies the notion of 'we' not just 'me' in
leadership & business. Pragmatic and practical, it provides a synthesis of techniques and process gained from
significant hands-on experience and notable business academics alike. Successful companies need to get clarity
and alignment on who they are and what they want to be – *The Business Battlecard* skillfully provides a process
to those looking for such guidance.

     Intelligent use of skills, imagination and time has never been more relevant for future prosperity. So is it
a time to rely wholly on your instincts to start anew or perhaps let a little of the outside in? Paul's book provides
a process and framework to help businesses on their way – followed well it will provide answers to questions
too poignant to ignore."
Ed Cordin, Consulting Director, IDC EMEA

"Extremely good distillation of frameworks, templates and practical roadmaps for planning and implementing
'go-to-market' business strategies. Has a very high ROI"
Wasim Azhar, Lecturer in Marketing Stanford University and University of California, Berkeley

"*The Business Battlecard* starts out by asking the kinds of questions that most of us know are important, but don't ask ourselves often enough. It then provides a mechanism to answer the questions.

Based on work with a wide range of customers over many years, the concepts and exercises in the book have the ring of authenticity to them. You can always tell when someone has actually been directly involved with a topic, and when they are merely repeating the 'right' answer. Paul has obviously been through difficult times with key customers, he's assisted them to articulate and then execute on fundamental concepts, and now, with *The Business Battlecard*, he is sharing his experience with a wider group. Who could have thought that discussing strategy could be this much fun?"
Larry Chisvin, COO, Nasdaq quoted, PLX Technology, CA, USA

"Without a solid go-to-market strategy in place, nothing layered on top—not a sales methodology, nor a partnership strategy, nor a marketing campaign – will get the job done. In *The Business Battlecard*, Paul serves up a practical solution, from soup to nuts – the step-by-step, proven path on which the senior management team can collaborate to ensure every step taken is not only forward, but a step in the right direction. This book is a 'must use' for every small company CEO."
Dave Stein, CEO ES Research & featured sales columnist Sales and Marketing Management Magazine, USA.

"Paul O'Dea's new book, *The Business Battlecard*, fully delivers on its opening pledge – to 'show you how to devise a clear strategy to grow your business; get your team aligned around it; and execute it'.

Strategy is the keyword throughout. A clear strategy that the whole company – not just the exec team – unites around, is absolutely vital for a growing company. Leaders of growing companies will find Paul's new book a concise, clear and very usable 'Battlecard' for strategy creation, execution and continual improvement as they grow their businesses."
Kieran Conlon, Regional Vice President Sales Europe, Globoforce

"Reading *The Business Battlecard* an old Japanese proverb kept coming to mind: 'Vision without action is a daydream. Action without vision is a nightmare'. This book helps you avoid the nightmare scenario by turning your vision into an executable strategy that will deliver value to your customers and grow your company. Sustaining growth is a constant battle and effective strategies that are well targeted and easily understood are crucial to winning this battle. So it's apt that Paul has used the term 'Battlecard' to describe his innovate approach to the strategy creation process."
Barry Murphy, Vice President, Business Development, Oracle Communications Global Business Unit

"There are books that tell you what to do and there are books that show you what to do. This book shows you what to do. It gives you the simple, practical tools which you need to manage and grow your business.

After reading some business books, I come away thinking: What should I do next? How should I do it? This book starts there – it shows you 'what to do next' in a very simple, easy to use framework that doesn't require expensive consultants to do the implementation!"
Riaz Merchant, President, Mertech Data Systems, FL, USA

Published by
Oak Tree Press
19 Rutland Street, Cork, Ireland
www.oaktreepress.com

A catalogue record of this book is
available from the British Library.

ISBN 978-1-904887-28-7

Printed in Ireland by Nicholson & Bass
Design by hexhibit.com

THE BUSINESS BATTLECARD

Winning Moves for Growing Companies

Paul O'Dea

Acknowledgements

Many people, companies, advisors and academics have influenced the content in this book, none more so than the CEOs of growing companies, whom I have had the privilege of working with in the years since moving from entrepreneur to 'strategy consultant'. Their challenges, stories and experiences guided me throughout to focus on delivering a book that was 'usable'.

Thanks to the people working at companies mentioned in the book, like Salesforce.com, Google, Prêt à Manger, Zara... you set great examples to draw on.

I am particularly grateful to all those who reviewed early drafts and whose honest feedback and encouragement made this a far better book. There are listed here in alphabetical order: Wasim Azhar, Tammy Billington, Richard Bryce, Joe Callery, Bernie Cullinan, Donal Daly, Paul Dooley, Ina Foley, Justine Emoe, Jackie Fitzgerald, James and Charlotte Helm, Colin Hughes, Maeve Kneafsey, Walter Kuemmerle, Claire Mc Bride, Bill McCarthy, Cormac MacFhionnlaoich, John Nolan, John O'Shea and Dave Stein.

Particular thanks to my colleague, at Select Strategies, Emer O'Donnell who made an immense contribution and helped refine many of the key ideas. Major thanks to Bridget Hourican, a great editor, who I couldn't recommend highly enough. She improved this book's flow and content greatly. Special thanks are due to Alastair Keady whose insightful approach produced excellent graphics from rough ideas.

The following also provided invaluable assistance:

• Numerous people I've worked with in Enterprise Ireland and the Dublin Institute of Technology. They acted as sounding boards, provided feedback, and generously offered great insights.

• Sean O'Sullivan, who graciously wrote the foreword.

• Donal Daly, CEO of The TAS Group, with whom I co-authored Select Selling, a source for some of the ideas and content in this book.

• Brian O'Kane, of publishers Oak Tree Press, who provided excellent guidance and encouragement.

• Emer Burton, who did early research work.

• Steve and Nicola Eustace, Peter Haran, Pat Moran, Helen O'Reilly and the others who climbed Carrantuhill and taught me about basecamps.

Finally to my wife Clare (and chief editor) whose contribution I am proudest to acknowledge – your support and guidance has been invaluable. To Sean, Maria and Ross – each of you made your contributions and yes, Dad's book is finished!

To my Dad, Paddy.

FOREWORD

Entrepreneurs and business leaders never act alone. Success, when it comes, is built brick by brick upon a foundation of believers, supporters, teammates, customers, and family and friends. In the early days – and through the trying nights – of doubts and contradictions, the struggle of building a business is made easier by supporters labouring side-by-side with you to make the great dream come alive.

In this book, Paul O'Dea gives you the tools to earn that support. By gaining the advantage of a clear and concise 'battlecard', you stand ready to get your team firing all its bullets at the same target. There is nothing like a unified team to make the infinite challenges in building a business seem surmountable, because with a unified team, those challenges are surmountable. And there is nothing that excites customers more than clear vision and clear leadership.

Unlike many authors, Paul understands that leadership may begin with an individual, but if it ends there, very little of value is created. In this book, he highlights the importance of the team in 'forming and norming' around the Business Battlecard.

True leadership is not the oft-imagined lone entrepreneur/manager making every decision and being the sole creative force, but instead is an empowering collaboration of team talent. True leadership isn't about creating followers. It's about creating leaders.

I have spent over twenty years starting, building, managing – and mismanaging – a wide variety of businesses, mostly in the technology sector, ranging from companies that employed a handful of people to organizations that employed thousands. Several of these have succeeded, several have failed. What I know for sure is that American writer James Oppenheimer had it right: "The foolish man seeks happiness in the distance, the wise grows it under his feet".

What you'll learn in this book are specific ways you can work with your team to get everyone fully engaged in the process of refining the vision for your company, defining your markets, and sticking to the mission.

Strategy must be acted out here and now, rather than put off to a far corner, as a dusty notecard tacked up onto a wall, or the goal of some future quarter. It must be as vibrantly alive and powerful as a football match or an action movie, and evident in the daily actions of the entire staff of your company.

Most start-up businesses are not necessarily happy places throughout all their phases. Fun places, they can be. Challenging, certainly. But happiness comes when people and teams converge to produce results, to guard each other's backs – to bump, set and spike each other's points to victory. This only happens in the aligned team.

Patience and persistence are what it takes to become a world leader in your chosen field. As Dr. Seuss might have put it: 'Yes you can, you can indeed, build great products and a market lead. You will win in business and soar to heights, have victorious battles and fight great fights.'

But it takes more than dreams to get there. It takes an absolute dedication; a ruthlessly simple and repetitive honing of a competitive advantage and strategy.

Somewhere after the start but before the business has 'made it', there comes the darkness: a point where nothing is certain, where in-fighting or finger-pointing frequently occur, where a customer pulls out or a financial crisis starts. If Thomas Paine had tried to start a business and not a revolution, he would have said that these are the times that try men's souls. In mythology, it's called the hero's journey. And it is at this time when your strategy is most needed, to make it through to the other side. The journey may be long. It will be hard. But if it ends in triumph, its rewards defy imagining.

Then again, for business purposes, perhaps that should be called the 'heroes' journey' – plural. For there is never one hero in the creation of a great business, but many, acting in concert.

Paul and I met through a board on which we both serve. I hope you find in this book what I have found in Paul himself: a trusted advisor and confidant. Sharp insight combined with smooth, clarifying process.

Good luck in battle. May your journey be heroic, and your strategy sound.

Sean O'Sullivan
Kinsale, Ireland
December 2008

Sean O'Sullivan is general manager of *Avego*, executive chairman of *Mapflow*, and runs *SOSventures*, a $100 million venture capital fund. He was a founder of *MapInfo Corporation*, *NetCentric Corporation*, *JumpStart International*, and is an award-winning documentary filmmaker.

- → **Introduction**
- ↘ **Commit to a Shared Vision**
- ↘ **Select your Sweet Spot Customer**
- ↘ **Create Measurable Value**
- ↘ **Beat the Competition**
- ↘ **Crack the Channel Code**
- ↘ **Execute The Business Battlecard™**

'Tactics without strategy is the noise before defeat.'

Sun Tsu, Art of War

When we started out advising companies, we met the CEO of a growing company, who was trying to put in place a strategy to drive his company forward. By nature an enthusiastic, energetic individual, he brought all his daunting force and thoroughness to the task, first acquiring top business and strategy books, then devising numerous business plans, then getting the consultants in.

But things weren't going as he hoped. The task of strategy creation wasn't responding to his energy and commitment the way other areas of his life did. The books were piling up on his desk; discarded business plans overflowed on the office floor; the suit-clad consultants spoke soothingly in incomprehensible jargon. Every time he thought he had a good strategy in place, he'd start to explain it to his team, only to have their puzzled questions pick it apart. Sessions with the board became fraught, as he sensed their lack of confidence and unspoken disappointment.

He felt adrift – was it his fault or was something more fundamental to blame? His team avoided reading his business plans the way kids avoid homework. The sheer weight of his books and plans was crushing him. Worst of all, the company wasn't growing, because he'd no idea what direction he was taking it in.

Finally, like water coming to boiling point, or the Hulk tearing out of his shirt, he'd had enough. Being a man of action, he put a clear line through this hapless, confused, humiliating period of his life. He took down all his strategy books and all his business plans, made a bonfire in his back garden, and ceremoniously *burnt them*.

"From now on," he said, "I want a strategy you can see on *one page*. If you can't get it down on one page, it's no good to me."

This made a huge impression on us. We realised that brevity is not just the soul of wit, but the soul of strategy.

In today's hectic, multi-tasking business climate, no-one has time to read through weighty strategy tomes, no-one has time to devise long, complicated business plans, no-one has time to take their busy team through complex jargon and labyrinthine arguments, or their impatient board through vague proposals for immeasurable growth.

What you have in your hands is, of course, a strategy book and, yes, it's 125 pages, but we promise that you will come away from reading this with a targeted strategy **on one page** which will help you grow your business.

In our experience – and in the experience of the fed-up CEO who burnt his books – strategies fail because they're too complicated, too disjointed or because they're never implemented.

"From now on," he said, "I want a strategy you can see on one page. If you can't get it down on one page, it's no good to me."

Brevity is not just the soul of wit, but the soul of strategy.

Some companies fail at the outset and never begin to get strategy underway; others fail at the half-way mark because they can't see where all this is going, and others fail at the last hurdle because they have their strategy down on paper but they never implement it.

So our pledge is that this book will show you how to devise a clear strategy to grow your business; get your team aligned around it; and execute it.

Mindful of that stressed-out CEO, we focus throughout on being pragmatic, clear, user-friendly, and inclusive. This is a book for the whole team, not just for the CEO. Because the team works through this strategy together, they are less likely to pick it apart. We break strategy down into five handy components, or tools, which are integrated on one PowerPoint.

Why a strategy?

But first, the crucial question – why create a strategy?

Strategy creation requires time and effort from the whole team. Why bother? Why not just continue focusing on the tasks in hand, which are certainly demanding enough?

But think about what you're up against: it's a buyer's market. You face trenchant competition and the pool of customers isn't that large. Shareholders want growth. Resources are limited and cash flow is tight – especially, let's face it, in the current economic climate. Your team make a lot of demands, and don't seem to share the same priorities.

How are you going to get through this without a strategy? In today's competitive climate, growing a company is a bit like waging a war, which is why we've called our one-page strategy plan, the Battlecard. Like a general, you have to fully understand what your competitors are doing and what your customers want. You have to keep your own troops armed, fed and disciplined, and of course you have to pay close attention to external conditions.

No-one goes to war without a carefully worked-out strategy, and you shouldn't either. Strategy is particularly important for growing companies because they're sniping and trying to gain ground from the bigger, more established companies. Where large companies can afford to batten down the hatches, growing companies have to think in terms of guerrilla warfare.

You don't have to be an expert on growing companies to know that they are fraught with risk. Even so, our research for this book led to hair-raising findings. Many growing companies have good financial, legal, production and sales processes but non-existent, or weak strategy creation processes. This has resulted in an epidemic of weak strategies, which are preventing growth.

What about your company? Are you suffering growing pains? If so, you have probably

blamed the sales team or the product – or both. But is something else at fault?

A huge number of companies start out well – they have an interesting product, which finds buyers, and an enthusiastic team. But then they hit a glass ceiling. Their management teams can't understand why – they have good people, all the market data, and internal processes, like accounting and quality, are in place. Yet, instead of growing they're still bumping their noses off the ceiling.

When you look at how such companies operate, you realise that they respond to situations in an ad hoc way; they tend to say yes to every opportunity because they're scared to turn down revenue; as a result they spread themselves thin, and start carrying out tasks that they're not particularly qualified to do and not particularly interested in. They devalue their reputation and inhibit growth, and all because they've never put in place a coherent, logical, unifying strategy.

Nothing prevents growth more than a weak strategy, nothing drives growth faster than a superior one. If you're heading in the wrong direction, then going faster or worker harder only makes things worse. Companies that develop winning strategies understand their customers more profoundly than their customers understand themselves. They anticipate their competitors' moves. They articulate an inspirational vision, which is clearly understood by even the most junior member of the team.

Nothing prevents growth more than a weak strategy, nothing drives growth faster than a superior one.

The five battlecard questions

Our strategy approach is based entirely on growing companies. Through working with over 250 growing companies in the US and Europe, we have identified the factors which accelerate and inhibit growth. Our insights are based on the workshops we have conducted over the years, and on validation from world class CEOs and members of the venture community, who helped us refine our approach.

Our aim throughout has been to keep strategy creation simple and strong. Of course it also needs to be comprehensive. Because strategy can be daunting, it's advisable to break it down, just as large-scale wars are broken down into battles and skirmishes.

So what are the 'battles' in business strategy? We work with diverse companies, from different sectors, but insofar as they all need to grow in a competitive environment, they all face similar challenges. In our experience, all companies, regardless of sector, have to deal with the following five areas:

- Company vision (including mindset);
- Customers;
- Value (not just the value of product/service, but also of staff, sales partners etc);

- Competition;
- The Channels used to get products to market (a much wider choice since the arrival of the internet).

These five areas are the battlegrounds where companies wage war, and we've used them to craft the five questions on which our approach is centred:

- **What** do you want to be famous for?
- **Who** are your selected customers?
- **Where** is your measurable value?
- **Why** should customers choose you rather than your competitors?
- **How** will you get your product to market?

We believe that at the root of weak strategies is a failure to address these five questions. This results in confused product development teams, disillusioned sales people and limited revenue growth.

None of these questions exists in isolation. All are strongly linked, to the extent that the answer to one question strongly determines the answer to another. Without being clear on what you want to be famous for, how can you be clear on the value you offer? Your customers choose you over the competition because of the value you deliver and because the route you take to market suits them. If you modify that value, or change the route, you'll have to consider changing customers, or incentivising existing ones to accept your new direction.

Successful companies can answer these questions. They're on-message. All of the areas of their business are working together in a **virtuous circle**, which is a concept we explore in Chapter 6, **Executing the Business Battlecard**. The teams of unsuccessful companies, faced with these questions, retreat in disarray. They're in a vicious circle.

Try the following experiment: get your team together and ask them to answer the five questions.

If all their answers are exactly the same, then congratulations, your team is aligned. But we seldom come across a company where everyone had the same answers from the outset! More likely is that you get radically different answers – Marketing might see value in promotions, Engineering in the product features, Finance may want to improve margin, while the CEO dreams of accelerated growth.

Misalignment won't help you beat the competition. It's like being the coach of a rowing team, which doesn't synchronise their strokes – team performance is under par and you don't win as often as you should.

Think about the cost and impact of this alignment problem. Clearly your team is not as productive as they should be. Your sales people may not be calling on the right customers. Your marketing team may not be clear on your message. Product teams may not be delivering in a way that helps beat the competition. Your company's performance starts looking like the slower moving tankers that are your bigger competitors.

THE SOLUTION – The Business Battlecard™

Unlike the command and control structure of yesterday, where the leadership team decided on strategy, today's knowledge worker is at the coalface. She is closer to customers and closer to the latest ideas. As part of the small team of a growing company, she is very likely multi-tasking – trying to achieve sales targets one day, measuring value the next. In short, she is now creating, rather than following, strategy.

Creating strategy is – or should be! – fun, and it's one of the reasons why talented people choose to work in growing companies – because they want to make a difference, and to feel that they are responsible for the company's direction, not just following orders.

But they also want to see fast results and to feel that they're moving forward in a targeted way. If there's a sense of drift, they'll go back to following orders. They want a strategy that's clear, simple, comprehensive, and that enables them to react quickly to new opportunities and new difficulties; a strategy which they understand completely, because they helped create it.

Distilled on to one PowerPoint, the **Business Battlecard** is designed to drive growth through the glass ceiling. It makes strategy creation a continuous process owned not just by top management, but by the whole company. By its title, it signals that growing companies are fighting a 'war' on several fronts: the battle against competitors, the battle for customers' minds, the battle for investors' wallets, the battle for employees' hearts.

Growing companies are fighting a 'war' on several fronts: the battle against competitors, the battle for customers' minds, the battle for investors' wallets, the battle for employees' hearts.

You and your team craft the **Battlecard** through the exercises, interactive workshops and graphical tools laid out in this book. This approach facilitates discussion, keeps focus on the Five Questions, and injects fun into the process. Strategy creation is a time for your team to put aside immediate concerns and focus on the bigger picture – what kind of company do you want to build and which direction should it take? Strategy creation shouldn't be like cramming for exams, it should have the excitement and urgency of generals preparing for battle.

The discipline of debating and crafting strategy forces you to select what's really important. Your Business Battlecard clarifies what you stand for – and what you don't.

The discipline of debating and crafting strategy forces you to select what's really important. Your **Business Battlecard** clarifies what you stand for – and what you don't. It combines high-level strategic principles with our practical experience of advising growing companies. It brings strategy into mainstream management discussions, rather than leaving it for crisis times or annual planning sessions.

Business Battlecard™
Winning moves for growing companies

1 SHARED VISION
What do you want to be famous for?

2 SWEET SPOT
Who are your selected customers?

5 CHANNELS
How will you get your product to market?

3 MEASURABLE VALUE
Where is your measurable value?

4 BEAT THE COMPETITION
Why should customers choose you rather than your competitors?

The Business Battlecard is a trademark of Select Strategies.

On the Battlecard, you'll see five sections, which we call 'tools'. Each tool is differentiated by colour, and is linked to one of our five questions. The pie chart in the centre of the Battlecard emphasizes the interdependence of the tools, and drives home the alignment between the five questions. We call this piechart the **virtuous circle**. The mountain in the top right hand corner symbolizes your goals and aspirations (the summit of your ambitions), which will only be achieved by following a carefully planned ascent, broken down into phases, or basecamps, where you review, recalculate and recalibrate your strategy.

The first five chapters of the book correspond to the five tools, and each tool is introduced and explained in its relevant chapter. In the sixth chapter, we show you how to integrate the five tools on to the **Business Battlecard**, and how to set basecamps.

The five tools on the Business Battlecard, linked to the five questions, are:

- **Commit to a shared vision**: What do you want to be famous for?
- **Select your sweet spot customer**: Who are your selected customers?
- **Create measurable value**: Where is your measurable value?
- **Beat the competition**: Why should customers choose you rather than your competitors?
- **Crack the channel code**: How will you get your product to market?

Chapter 1, **Commit to a shared vision**, creates the framework for your strategy. By asking the question what do you want to be famous for?, it encourages you to think about your values and why you think your company is special. It shows you how to craft a shared vision, through identifying the company mindset and the unique skills which you offer.

Chapter 2, **Select your sweet spot customer**, defines your ideal target customers and those you should avoid. Case studies show how growing companies accelerated their revenues by concentrating their energies on 'ideal profile' prospects, instead of using the 'spray and pray' approach so often adopted.

Chapter 3, **Create measurable value** addresses the question of creating, delivering and measuring value. By carefully examining your customers' key challenges, you will develop new insights into creating value. On the basis that unproven value goes unrewarded, we show you how to measure the value you deliver.

Chapter 4, **Beat the competition** looks at why customers should choose you over competitors. In seeking to deliver superior value, many companies focus only on products or services, but you have the opportunity to differentiate from the moment customers decide they need a new solution, to the time when they decide to dispose of it. Examine all your company activities – including staffing, budgeting and sales partners – and refine them, so that you're delivering superior value at every step of the way.

Chapter 5, **Crack the channel code** looks at the question 'How will you get your product to market?' How do your ideal customers like to purchase, and what routes to market are available for your offering? This question, once relatively straightforward, has been revolutionised by the growth of the internet. Channels have become the new drivers of revenue growth. It's not what you sell but how you sell it.

Finally, Chapter 6, **Execute the Business Battlecard**, looks at integrating the five tools and executing the strategy. It shows how successful companies have all five tools working together in a **virtuous circle**, leading to growth.It also introduces you to the concept of **basecamps**, which are the time your team comes together to review strategy, to recalculate the risks, to check whether you're on the right path, and to prepare for the next phase of ascent.

Your completed **Business Battlecard** becomes your touchstone, helping to bring clarity, consistency and a common language to your team. It puts you on the path of continually improving and adapting your strategy, so that your team starts to fulfil its ambitions.

Workshopping the Business Battlecard

The Business Battlecard arose from workshops we've held with growing companies, and in our opinion the best way for you to use this book is as a basis for workshops on strategy creation. You can of course just read through, enjoy each chapter, and pick up tips, but to get full value, craft your strategy, and grow your company, it's best to get your team involved and to 'workshop' the book.

Generally speaking, you'll need to host a number of workshops to work through each tool and integrate them on the Battlecard. Get your team together, and provide each member with a copy of the book. Encourage them to read the relevant chapter before the workshop. Each chapter follows a similar structure: first, we outline the concepts involved; second, using case study material, we provide examples to illustrate the concepts. We highlight both well-known examples and examples from our own experience. In some cases we have named the company, whilst in others disguising their identity has allowed us to reveal more of their story. The names of disguised companies are italicised.

The 'cloudy' backdrop which runs throughout the book introduces questions specific to each chapter. Your team members might like to jot down answers to these questions as prep for the workshop.

At the workshop, create a sense of urgency and fun. Workshop discussions can be heated, as each team member tries to impose his or her view. It's important to have a convener – the CEO, or an outside facilitator. Fortunately the tools, which are the core of each workshop, provide a focal point. Completing them helps resolve arguments.

The facilitator will benefit from doing prep in advance of the workshops. He or she should talk to customers, competitors and industry experts to try and get a full picture of what it takes to win in the sector. The secret to workshop success is good preparation.

Blank full page versions of the tools are available at the back of the book and electronic versions are available at **www.selectstrategies.com**.

Someone once asked the guy sweeping the floor at space agency NASA during the Kennedy era what he was doing. He replied: "I'm helping put a man on the moon." This story may be apocryphal but it illustrates what we're saying here, and one of the reasons why we wrote this book. Strategies work when the message is clear and when the whole team feels ownership of it.

What distinguishes successful companies from the unsuccessful? What binds companies as diverse as Ryanair, Lexus, and Salesforce? It's that everyone working for them is on-message and pulling together, and their vision can be articulated clearly and concisely – not just by the CEO, but by the guy sweeping the floor.

Eventually, by working through the tools presented in this book, that CEO who burnt his books, got his strategy down on one page – his Battlecard. He stuck it on the wall behind his desk. Now, when presented with a new situation – such as a set of potential new customers, or a proposed new product, or a potential new sales partner – he and his team check together, via the Battlecard, that the new situation is on-strategy. If it is, they go with it; if not, they say no. As a result the company is growing in a calm, targeted manner. There is no drift, distraction, or devaluation. They're heading straight for the moon, not disappearing into black holes.

Now read on to find out how to achieve this for your company.

- ↘ **Introduction**
- ⊘ **Commit to a Shared Vision**
- ↘ **Select your Sweet Spot Customer**
- ↘ **Create Measurable Value**
- ↘ **Beat the Competition**
- ↘ **Crack the Channel Code**
- ↘ **Execute The Business Battlecard™**

'A shared vision is not an idea... It is, rather, a force in people's hearts, a force of impressive power. It may be inspired by an idea, but once it goes further – if it is compelling enough to acquire the support of more than one person – then it no longer exists as an abstraction; it becomes palpable.'

(Peter Senge), *The Fifth Discipline, The Art and Practice of the Learning Organization* (1990)

Alfred Hitchcock was once asked what his vision was in making movies, he replied: "simply to scare the hell out of everybody".

In pursuit of scaring the hell out of us, Hitchcock virtually created the thriller genre, and pioneered techniques to keep viewers on the edge of their seats: inventive camera angles, electronic scores, twists in the tale, even a Dali dream sequence.

Hitchcock had his own vision but film is a collaborative process – he could never have scared the hell out of everybody without the help of the sound engineers, cinematographers, actors, composers, art directors, lighting designers, dolly grips and tea ladies. He worked with the best in the business and because he could communicate exactly what he wanted, they gave him their best.

Growing a successful company is a lot like making a brilliant movie. Like Hitchcock, you need to have a shared vision of the direction you are taking, distinctive competencies to help you do it, and a great team with the same mindset.

Why a Shared Vision?

In the absence of a shared vision, the employees tend to pursue their own, short-term goals. They pull in different directions and set different priorities – the predictable result is friction, pettiness and, ultimately, chaos.

Very often, a company is founded because somebody wants to work for themselves or spots an opportunity to build something and make money. That person then sets up with a number of former colleagues and, in the early, heady days, a few big customers are reeled in. The company expands, and more people are employed. But, in the absence of a properly formulated and communicated shared vision, the employees tend to pursue their own, short-term goals. They pull in different directions and set different priorities – the predictable result is friction, pettiness and, ultimately, chaos.

Put simply, in Peter Senge's words, a shared vision is "a force in people's hearts, a force of compelling power... a deep purpose that expresses the organisation's reason for existence". It defines your company's direction and provides inspiration for the whole team, setting guidelines as to what your company should and should not do.

Every important decision, from target customer selection, to how you choose to deliver superior value for your customers, should be taken in the light of your shared vision. Shared vision sets out what you are striving to achieve, provides direction and guidance for your team, and signposts the direction that your Business Battlecard should take. Without commitment to a shared vision, it is difficult to craft a winning strategy – indeed we are convinced that lack of commitment to a shared vision is one of the reasons that so many strategies fail.

Growing companies with limited money and resources may have nothing to offer but their dream. Your shared vision must be compelling and have the power to inspire and mobilise your entire company in the interests of a common purpose. Your task is to create a shared vision that will engage the company towards its goal. John F. Kennedy's vision of 'putting a man on the moon' captured the imagination of millions of Americans in 1961 to do just that. Within eight years, the dream had been achieved.

Where Do You Start?

Let's face it, many company visions are boring. Often, they appear to fit a formula designed for the company website – rather than genuinely reflecting a true vision of the future.

> *"The visions of exceptional leaders are.... compelling and pull people toward them. Intensity coupled with commitment is magnetic. These intense personalities do not have to coerce people to pay attention: they are so intent on what they are doing that, like a child completely absorbed with creating a sandcastle in a sandbox, they draw others in."* – Warren Bennis.

Intense personalities do not have to coerce people to pay attention: they are so intent on what they are doing that, like a child completely absorbed with creating a sandcastle in a sandbox, they draw others in

Well of course Warren Bennis is right but it's hard for most of us to have a 'man on the moon' vision and ambition. It is not easy to lift your head from day-to-day operational issues and firefighting. Too many companies spend too much time in the trenches, fighting hand-to-hand with competitors, and sapping energy to gain a few feet of progress, often won with a new product feature, a new service or a special price reduction.

Benefiting humanity: Merck

In the 1920s, long before it became fashionable to write about vision, George Merck expressed his shared vision of Merck as **"a world-class company, benefiting humanity through innovative contributions to medicine"**. This vision was based on a mindset of integrity, contribution to society, responsibility to customers and employees and the pursuit of quality. *Merck* transformed itself from a manufacturer of chemical products into one of the world's leading pharmaceutical companies by an unshaken adherence to its vision, which remains almost identical 80 years on.

Your shared vision should light a fire in the bellies of your team, grip stakeholders and be explicable in simple language. It should answer questions like: What are we trying to build or create? What will success look like? What is our shared picture of the future? What are we going to be famous for?

Some companies accidentally discover their shared vision. They start off just doing stuff, selling products that people want and they build their vision around their success. eBay is a good case in point.

Connecting everyone on the planet: eBay

eBay founder, Pierre Omidyar, wanted to create a "fair and equitable market, where all users could have access to similar information". Using his $30-a-month home internet service, he set up eBay in 1995. Charging a small fee for listing and a percentage of the final auction price, Omidyar's success came quickly. In the first month he took in $1,000 and revenue doubled monthly from that point on, with brand awareness coming mostly via word-of-mouth.

Two years after founding eBay, Omidyar attracted Benchmark Capital, which initially invested $6.5 million (a stake subsequently worth more than $1 billion). On 24 September 1998, eBay went public and Omidyar and colleagues found themselves wealthy beyond belief. eBay's shared vision is "to make eBay the place where everybody on the planet can do business with anyone else on the planet".

Don't confuse shared vision with a tagline or marketing slogan. Too often companies' stated visions are embarrassing sets of self-conscious words, crafted for a business plan or website, that nobody remembers and would feel uncomfortable having to repeat. Hitchcock, Merck's and Omidyar's visions were heartfelt and authentic. They weren't trying to think of catchy slogans, they were articulating their deepest needs, and they came up with strong, personal words.

In this chapter, we provide a process and guidelines that you can use with your team to craft a shared and compelling vision for the future of your company.

A shared vision includes:
- **Mindset**: This answers the question, 'How do we do things round here?' What are the thinking patterns that drive and guide behaviour in your company?
- **Distinctive competencies**: What are you really good at? Better at than the competition? What are your unique strengths that help you deliver superior value to customers?
- **Stretch objectives**: What will your company look like in three years? What will success look like? What concrete goals have you set for revenue, customers, staffing, and offerings?
- A **Shared Vision Statement**, which is bold, authentic, and strongly communicable.

Getting a team committed to a shared vision is challenging. Those that the vision needs to appeal to – shareholders, CEO, sales, finance, and engineering – are all coming from different perspectives. Many attempts at crafting shared visions flounder through lack of follow through, not being grounded in reality, or being so far-fetched that most people in the company just go back to business as usual. The process described in this chapter is based on our experience in facilitating workshops with growth companies, and builds upon work done by Peter Senge and Jim Collins (author of *Good to Great*).

The Shared Vision Tool

↘ Shared Vision Tool

◉ ● ● ● ● = ◔

⊙ MINDSET
How do you do things around here?

⊕ STRETCH OBJECTIVES
What do we want to build?

⊙ DISTINCTIVE COMPETENCIES
What are you really good at?

Customer

Stretch Objectives

Product

People

Finance

Shared Vision Statement

The Shared Vision Tool is the first of the five tools we will work through in the book. The five tools all come together in summary form in your **Business Battlecard** in Chapter 6.

To get you in the right frame of mind for thinking about vision, here's a kick-off exercise, which we find an excellent ice-breaker at workshops:

'What do you want to be famous for?'

Divide into small teams and ask each team to pick their favourite business publication – for example, *Business Week* or a relevant industry publication. then ask them to pretend they are journalists, writing an article about your company for the front page of their chosen publication in five years' time. Encourage the teams to craft headlines giving some news of the company – say, *'Company wins 100th customer'* or *'Company recognised by industry peers as leader in market'*. This exercise helps tap into people's best hopes for the future. Get the group to stretch their imaginations – don't let them be constrained by practical concerns, or by wondering how this might be achieved. Ask them what they want the company to be famous for. What type of place will your company be to work in? What types of products might you have? What will your sales figures be? What anecdotes illustrate how you got to this point? Encourage the team to use sub headlines, quotes from leading industry figures, industry statistics. Make the exercise fun. Use pictures. Finally, ask the different teams to present back their cover stories to the group. Draw the ideas out after the presentations. Seek ideas that might become part of the shared vision. Look for big 'ah ha' moments.

This exercise helps to create a sense of energy and commitment. It takes people away from day-to-day constraints, and helps them start to envisage a compelling future. Stick your magazine cover story on the wall to provide inspiration, as you work through the shared vision process.

Mindset – How Do You Do Things Around Here?

Your company's mindset comprises the few but important core ways of thinking and acting every day. Mindset comes from within. It is part of your company's DNA. A growing company's mindset is made up from a combination of ambition and core values. Unlike strategies, your mindset is relatively unchanging over time. Yet company mindset and strategy need to be aligned for growth.

Mindset cannot be copied from other successful companies or hashed out on the basis of what is good for sales. Industry sector, company history and the personal history of the senior management all contribute to mindset. Your company mindset should translate into behaviour, and should answer the question: "How do you do things around here?" A clear mindset is important to those working in the company as it is their guiding principle.

Each new team member needs to understand and be comfortable with the company's mindset before they take the job; otherwise the mindset gets diluted and the company's DNA isn't passed on. Or the new hire finds that they have taken a job in a company which doesn't suit them and whose goals they don't share. This is a serious waste of time and resources, both for the individual and the company.

Newcomers to the company will seek answers to questions like: what is important around here? What do I need to do to get respect and get ahead? What does the company leadership really reward, rather than what they say they reward?

A client of ours, had a great market opportunity but the co-founders had no agreed mindset. The vice president, sales director and chief technology officer were straining at the leash to grow the company tenfold. But the CEO was holding them back. He was already financially successful, and at 48 was cruising to retirement. For our client that meant one thing: if growth was the mindset, the CEO had to go!

Everyone involved in a growing company knows that personal and business goals are closely connected. Consciously reflect on your personal goals – first individually and then as a team. Think about the sacrifices you will have to make and how they will impact on others. Are you willing and able to adapt to change? Are you prepared to hire people better than yourselves to run the company as it grows? Are you prepared to relinquish control?

Build a company with a clear mindset and good things will happen. If the founder's only desire is to win big deals and sell the company to the highest bidder, the employees will notice. Talented people will move on to a company that offers a sense of common purpose. It is rarely just about money.

Your mindset must be authentic. It must be lived, rather than flowing from a copywriter's pen. The CEO and the management team must embody this mindset and lead by example. Your mindset should translate into how your team acts, and onwards into the experience you provide your customers.

Your mindset may include beliefs about how you treat people, the types of products you aspire to build, how you contribute to society or how you deal with customers. Your mindset should comprise four or five deeply held beliefs – they are the few but important things that your company is passionate about.

For example, if your company's mindset is 'the customer is king', then for this to be authentic, you would expect to see the following: the whole team knows what it takes for your selected customers to recommend you to others. You hire people with a mindset of 'customer is king' and often hire people from the ranks of your customers. Your senior management team spends a lot of time with customers. You have clear customer satisfaction metrics that are acted on. You respond fast to customer problems and tie some of your reward system to customer satisfaction. In essence the company mindset is manic about trying to exceed customers' expectations.

Each new team member needs to understand and accept the company's mindset before they take the job. Otherwise the core company mindset gets diluted with each new hire and the company loses its soul.

Ideas and innovations: *Toy Story*

There is a scene in *Toy Story* 2, where the old man repairing Woody tells the impatient toy collector, Al, 'You can't rush art'. This is, of course, true but according to Pixar, the company behind *Toy Story*, their animators also need the following mindset: everyone must have the freedom to communicate with anyone, it must be safe for everyone to offer ideas, and they must stay close to the latest innovations. The Pixar public expect to see something new every time – the flexible and dynamic mindset of the team helps the studio achieve this.

Other examples of mindset include Virgin Airline's premium on having a sense of fun and innovation. From its founder Richard Branson, you can imagine how this translates into behaviour such as being able to laugh at yourself, improving the customer experience through humour, showing enthusiasm on the job, creating a friendly environment and taking some risks.

Contrast this with a low cost airline, where cost-cutting is the mindset. One such airline has made it off limits for staff to charge their personal mobile phones at work. To many of us, that might seem excessively penny-pinching, but for employees there is a crystal clear understanding of the mindset of the company – a relentless attack on costs.

Being clear about mindset from the onset helps prevent drift. If mindset changes, it needs to do so consciously and be aligned with strategy, rather than changing ad hoc.

What are the top three things that are great about working for your company? What is really important to you?

Think of examples of behaviours that struck you in your company. Are there any famous company anecdotes?

What values would you never want to lose from your company? Which individuals in your company best embody your mindset?

What is your ambition for the company?

What needs to change in your mindset, going forward?

Distinctive Competencies – What are You Really Good At?

Distinctive competencies – such as world-class design from Bang & Olufsen, branding competence from Innocent, innovation competence from Dyson – help you win in your chosen market. They must be hard for your competitors to imitate. They must offer your customers superior value. They are areas you are going to invest in to become and stay a world leader. They will, if nurtured and invested in, fuel your growth. They go right across your company and will serve as the foundation for ways to beat the competition.

Examples of distinctive competencies include world-class design, branding, deep insight into customer needs, or staff who are particularly skilled, experienced or talented in a particular area. Having intellectual property or patents may give you an edge over competitors. Maybe your distinctive competence is the relentless pace and quality of your execution. You are just faster and better than anybody else at recognising, exploiting and delivering on market opportunities.

Many growth companies do a mix of things. They simply evolve and end up with different types of customers and a wide range of products. It's a recipe for mediocrity. It's too hard to try to grow several mini businesses at the one time – even by small increments per year. Companies that grow successfully understand what it takes to win in their chosen sector and also what they are really good at. They have the discipline and focus to build the right distinctive competencies. This clarity helps them select ideal customers, create measurable value, and beat the competition, all of which we discuss in later chapters.

Figure out what it takes to win in the market you are competing in. How is it changing? What will it take to win in your market in three years' time? What is happening that may change the rules of the game? What government regulations are coming down the tracks? What new capabilities can your suppliers provide that can help you deliver better value? How are your customer needs and perception of value changing? What markets can you win in and what markets can you not win in?

Your customers should recognise these distinctive competencies as valuable. The customer is the arbiter – if you are not able to convert a distinctive competence into superior value for the customer, then question whether it really is a distinctive competence. If your competitors already have these competencies or can easily acquire them, they are not distinctive.

Work out your distinctive competencies – you should have no more than two or three. Think about outsourcing or discontinuing some of the things that customers do not care about. Focus on the things that really create superior value.

Don't be a focus group of one – get advice. You may think that your staff, branding, or design are outstanding, but industry experts may not be impressed, customers may not

If you are not able to convert a distinctive competence into superior value for the customer, then question whether it really is a distinctive competence.

be willing to purchase, and competitors may not be worried.

Superior search solutions: *Google*

Google, internet search juggernaut, confounded the skeptics who argued that users would always switch around between search engines, rather than remaining loyal to one. Despite Google's relentless innovation, they remain largely true to their distinctive competence which is developing superior search solutions. And they hire the brightest people to help them do it. Google continues to refine, improve and invest in its distinctive competence and has blown its competitors out of the water.

A distinctive competence is something that is constantly invested in and improves over time. Winning companies figure out what they can do really well, and then they put resources behind that competence, and this accelerates growth. Figuring out your distinctive competencies isn't easy, but once done, you're on the path to beating the competition, something we address in more detail in Chapter 4, **Beat the Competition**.

What does it take to win in your sector?

What would independent industry experts say your distinctive competencies are?

What unique things do you do better than your competitors?

How hard are these for your competitors to copy?

How much do your customers value these competencies?

What new competencies do you need to develop?

Stretch Objectives

An all-encompassing shared vision like Hitchcock's or eBay's is great, but it needs to be supported by objectives in specific areas. Vision has to be made manageable, concrete, and broken down into goals that your team can readily envisage.

Stretch objectives are concrete goals in areas such as revenue, customers, people, product types or offerings. The objectives should stretch the team beyond what they believe today. They should be ambitious and include clear definitions of 'what success looks like' and specific timescales for achievement.

You should set stretch objectives across all company activities. For clarity, we divide these activities into four: Customer, Product, People, Finance. We use these terms throughout the book. 'Customer' is the responsibility of sales and marketing and customer support. 'Product' is your product, offering or professional service (such as consulting, or implementation) and is the responsibility of product management and engineering. 'People' is your staff and skills capability and is the responsibility of the leadership team. 'Finance' is accounts, shareholders and investors and is the responsibility of the CEO and CFO.

Here are questions to help you set stretch objectives for each key area. We generally use three years as the timeframe.

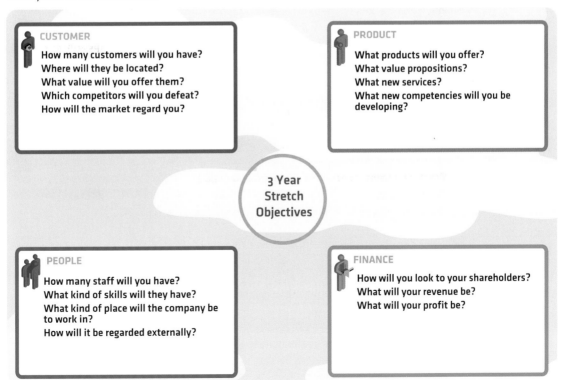

CUSTOMER
How many customers will you have?
Where will they be located?
What value will you offer them?
Which competitors will you defeat?
How will the market regard you?

PRODUCT
What products will you offer?
What value propositions?
What new services?
What new competencies will you be developing?

3 Year Stretch Objectives

PEOPLE
How many staff will you have?
What kind of skills will they have?
What kind of place will the company be to work in?
How will it be regarded externally?

FINANCE
How will you look to your shareholders?
What will your revenue be?
What will your profit be?

Shared Vision Statement

Articulating your vision in one statement serves as a lynchpin for your team. The statement is the final part of crafting your shared vision. It will probably take more than one sitting and shouldn't be forced. Shared vision comes in many sizes. Some statements are passionate rallying cries; others are practical and down-to-earth. Yours must be unique and should emerge from your mindset, distinctive competencies, and stretch objectives.

Examples of shared vision statements already given in this chapter are Hitchcock's 'simply to scare the hell out of everybody', eBay's 'the place where everybody on the planet can do business with anyone else on the planet' and Merck's 'a world-class company, benefiting humanity through innovative contributions to medicine'.

When NASDAQ-quoted Mentor Graphics was established, the company had, in the words of its founders, no articulated vision. The unarticulated vision was 'to build something people will buy'. After a few bruising encounters with a competitor seven times bigger, the company developed a shared vision that was simply 'Beat Daisy!' (their main competitor). This war-cry rallied the entire company in pursuit of a common purpose. Everyone knew what had to be done and they drove ahead with enthusiasm and determination. It gave them the boldness and will to succeed.

However, while a shared vision of beating a particularly feared competitor may galvanize commitment in the short term, it does not provide a long-term shared vision.

Instead, look for a company you admire in another niche and learn from their example. Your shared vision statement could then be as simple but as positive as: 'Be like X'. If you have a company with revenue of €5m, seek a role model with €50 million revenue. Learn how they achieved growth, what challenges they overcame and how they changed. Help your team paint the picture of 'Being like X'.

Your statement should be arresting, communicable and imaginable. It must be attractive to management, investors and employees. Stakeholders should be able to visualise it. 'We want to improve quality of life in Africa' is too vague but 'eliminating Aids in Africa' is concrete.

The kick-off exercise is an inspirational starting point. What do you want to be famous for? How high can you go in your sector? Below are some suggestions to help you craft your statement:

- Try opening with one of the following phrases:
  - 'Be like...'
  - 'Be recognized by the market as...'
    i.e. 'To be recognized by the market as the company that gave the power of SAP to one million small business by 2015'.

- Analogies or metaphors can help paint the picture, as in the hypothetical examples below:
  - Be the Amazon of pharmaceutical products
  - Be the Honda 50 of solar-powered motorbikes
  - Be the Virgin of shipping/bus transport
  - Be recognized by the market as global nanny for kids' mobile phones by 2011.

- Have a look at your stretch objectives. Think about making your shared vision defined, targeted and possibly timebound. Hitchcock's and eBay's visions weren't tied to a date, but we find that for growing companies a date can help make the statement less vague – for instance: 'To be recognized by the market as being in the top three companies in Europe in financial services IT outsourcing by 2012' is a better shared vision than 'to be the market leader in financial services IT outsourcing' and 'to win four gold medals in the 2016 Olympics' is a better shared vision for the Olympic Council of Ireland than just 'to win medals'.

Shared Vision Case Study
Eris, telecom software services

We recently facilitated a workshop with a company we'll call *Eris*. They are a telecoms software services company, with €15 million revenue and 20 mid-sized telecom operators as customers. *Eris* helps their customers bring low-level data into business performance dashboards, which senior telecom managers can use for decision-making purposes.

Eris were looking to break through to the next stage of growth but in their own words, 'were a bit stuck'. Engineering seemed to be pulling the company in one direction, sales in another and they were having a hard time with investors. The founder CEO was spending a lot of time balancing the polarised viewpoints around the management table.

Prior to a two day workshop, we spoke to the management team members individually, and to their customers, industry experts and board members to get a baseline objective assessment of 'where the company was'. This helped us gain insight into potential opportunities, *Eris'* ability to execute, performance gaps and what was inhibiting growth. We sensed that the company had lost its way and that its founding entrepreneurial spirit was dissipating.

What do you want to be famous for?
After presenting back our baseline assessment and to break the ice, we kicked off with the 'What do you want to be famous for?' exercise outlined earlier in the chapter. This caught the imagination, lifted tension and got the team thinking about the future in more than just financial terms.

Mindset

We then embarked on mindset – 'how do you do things around here?' The customer services manager argued that 'customer is king' was the mindset. Yet when we talked this through with the full group it quickly became clear that their mindset was more about *exceeding* customer expectations. We realized that 'Customer is king' had been set down because it was a handy slogan but that actually the company's behaviour was subtly different.

The CTO argued that the company needed to be at the bleeding edge of innovation or competitors would catch up. This mindset was eventually balanced with the consideration that whilst *Eris* would be responsible for the groundbreaking research, customers would have to pay for all development work. Their CEO argued that they should be leaders in their sector and have over 100 customers, rather than the 20 they had today. For this to be the case, the CTO felt that they needed to become a true product company, rather than a services company 'masquerading as a product company'. Finally mindset was chiseled out as follows:

- Consistently exceed customer expectations;
- Be at the bleeding edge of innovation – but be jointly funded by customers;
- Build products that solve the toughest network information problems for telecom operators.

Distinctive competencies

Then we looked at distinctive competencies. What competencies did they have that would help propel them towards their vision? What were they better than competitors at? Many of the claimed competencies were not distinctive at all. The first list was long – and needed to be refined considerably. We knew from our discussion with customers and industry experts that *Eris* was recognised by their industry as having both business and technical domain expertise in 'telecom operator network business intelligence'.

We finally agreed on two distinctive competencies:

- Patented tools in telecom operator network business intelligence;
- A world class team which spans business & IT expertise.

Three year Stretch Objectives

The next stage of the workshop took inspiration from the 'What do you want to be famous for?' exercise which had put the team into an ambitious frame of mind. Stretch objectives were debated around customer numbers and types; potential products and services; what kind of place *Eris* would be to work in, and on financial metrics that would indicate success.

The CEO felt success would only be achieved when they had more than 100 customers, with whom they were doing meaningful business. The VP sales was more focused on revenue and said his goal was €50 million in revenue; the CFO was focused on profits; the CTO on great products and being recognized as a great place to work... and so on. The key was to arrive at alignment around a set of balanced stretch objectives that the whole management team could buy into. They had to be ambitious enough to create some tension, but not completely unrealistic. Three year stretch objectives were agreed as follows:

- 50 customers with whom we conduct meaningful business;
- €50 million in revenue, with a 10 % net profit;
- Product-based company, with over 80% of revenue from product;
- Be recognised as the company of choice for the best in the industry to work in.

Shared Vision Statement

Finally, it was time to articulate their vision into one pithy statement. The statement emerged from the previous work. Words were interpreted and argued about. Finally the shared vision statement was agreed:

> To be recognised by the market in 2011 as one of the top three worldwide vendors for business intelligence solutions for telecom operators who have tough network information problems.

As one of the more sceptical participants told us afterwards, *"The Eris Shared Vision is now part of our DNA. It has become etched in our heads. The work on Shared Vision was painful for us all but it set the path for strategy creation and all our staff are clear as to what we are at".*

↘ Shared Vision Tool, *Eris, Telecoms Software*

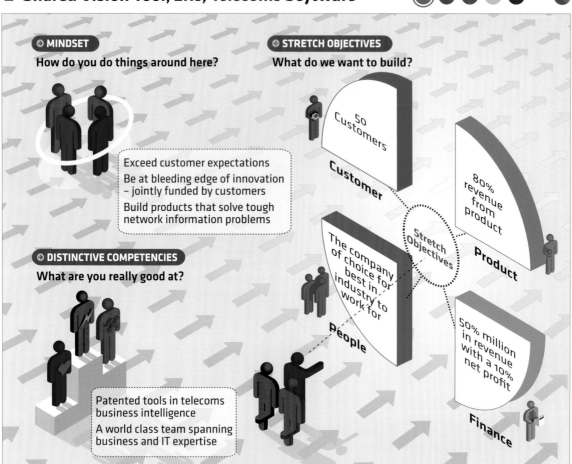

⊙ **MINDSET**

How do you do things around here?

Exceed customer expectations

Be at bleeding edge of innovation – jointly funded by customers

Build products that solve tough network information problems

⊙ **DISTINCTIVE COMPETENCIES**

What are you really good at?

Patented tools in telecoms business intelligence

A world class team spanning business and IT expertise

⊙ **STRETCH OBJECTIVES**

What do we want to build?

50 Customers

Customer

80% revenue from product

Stretch Objectives

The company of choice for best in industry to work for

Product

People

50% million in revenue with a 10% net profit

Finance

Shared Vision Statement

To be recognised by the market in 2011 as one of the top three worldwide vendors for business intelligence solutions for telecom operators who have tough network information problems

Use *Eris'* example to help you work through your own Shared Vision Tool. And finally, once you have your shared vision, preach the message like a mantra. As Winston Churchill put it:

'If you have an important point to make, don't try to be subtle or clever. Use the pile driver. Hit the point once. Then come back and hit it again. Then hit it a third time; a tremendous whack.'

↘ **Introduction**

↘ **Commit to a Shared Vision**

➔ **Select your Sweet Spot Customer**

↘ **Create Measurable Value**

↘ **Beat the Competition**

↘ **Crack the Channel Code**

↘ **Execute The Business Battlecard**™

"The customer is frequently wrong. We don't carry those sorts of customers. We write them and say: 'Fly someone else'."

Herb Kelleher, CEO, Southwest Airlines.

"This is too hard", said the stressed CEO of one of our client companies, let's call them *Mars*. "Every customer seems to want something a little bit different from our product. Most of these 'little differences' are taking months to build. The only thing our sales team cares about is commissions. I am getting it in the neck for our new product being six months late. I am spending my time on planes and with customers who are trying to make our product do things it was never designed to do. Our marketing team still doesn't understand our product and so they promote it as all things to all men. We seem to compete against different competitors in every deal. Our partners are dragging us into deals we should never be in. Our board only cares about numbers. It's impossible!"

Sound familiar? We spent some time with *Mars'* CEO and the rest of the founder team. *Mars* is a growing company with over €6 million annual revenue, based in Europe, with their sales team located in three international markets. We found that the company was heading into deep trouble, caused by 'headless chicken' behaviour and lack of a clearly-defined target customer. No discipline was being used to establish the segment of customers best suited to the company's product. The company was destroying its core product by trying to tailor it to too many different types of customers, who each had different needs. Revenue growth was about to stall. Many of the product team were disillusioned and on the verge of leaving. The sales and engineering relationship had broken down. Competitors were launching products with better functionality. It was critically urgent to focus energy and resource on finding a way out of this situation, starting with selecting their sweet spot.

In Chapter 1, you worked on getting your team committed to and aligned around a shared vision. This chapter focuses on the strategic importance of finding the 'sweet spot' – that point where your target customer selection leads to a perfect alignment of potential customers' needs and your distinctive competencies.

This chapter provides you with a process for filtering the market opportunity down so that you can focus your energy on those customers who most need your help.

Golfers will be familiar with the concept of a 'sweet spot'. It is the favoured spot on the clubface, where contact with the ball feels best. Those of you who play golf will be familiar with the feeling of not hitting the sweet spot – it doesn't 'feel' right, you don't get great distance, and generally your accuracy is way off. Hit the sweet spot and it feels good, you are in control of the ball, and that birdie is yours for the taking.

Finding the sweet spot is one of the most important processes you will ever undertake in your company. It could determine your company's success. If you rush to execute, before making the correct sweet spot decisions, you will waste time and valuable resources on the wrong customers. Like a golfer continually hacking out in the rough, you will expend a lot of energy but make little or no progress.

Few companies have products or services with broad appeal to all markets. Concentrating exclusively on those customers whose needs mirror the value you offer is critical to efficiency. Only where the wheels of your engine mesh smoothly with the cogs of the customer's power plant should you expend energy. This is your sweet spot: it's where all the forces align. The benefit you deliver to your customer is extreme. Adequate – but not extravagant – resource is expended to acquire the customer. Profitability increases. Customer satisfaction is high and the conversion rate of prospect to customer is greater than the norm.

Once you focus on your sweet spot customers, you will start to find that their needs will be similar. You will be asked the same questions in demonstrations. Each customer will start to feel like a carbon copy of the last. This is great news – since it allows you to get under the skin of the customer and to understand their business needs better than anybody else.

As one venture capitalist we work with, said:
> "I'd rather have a good team working with a focused sweet spot, than a great team working with a poorly defined sweet spot".

In many companies about 20% of customers generate 80% of the profit. Off-strategy customers can actually hinder growth because you're putting resources into an area where you have limited competence. Lack of a clearly defined sweet spot stunts growth.

Having a defined sweet spot allows you to configure your products, services and activities to deliver superior value to your customers – beating the competition, more often. Your messaging becomes tailored to that sweet spot, so that customers almost see themselves and self-select.

In this chapter we show how your company can grow revenue significantly by concentrating valuable energy on your sweet spot. We provide a sweet spot tool to help you define your target customers. Finding the sweet spot is all about focus – you will seldom see a company fail because it was too focused.

To start thinking about sweet spot, consider the following questions: What's preventing you focusing on winning more customers who fit your sweet spot? Consider those customers who love you, who promote your products without prompting – we call these gold customers – but why do they love you?

Like golf, finding the sweet spot is a continual battle. Nothing stays the same for very long. Market needs change and new competitors appear. But it is important to have an agreed process that helps you define and refine your sweet spot.

Only where the wheels of your engine mesh smoothly with the cogs of the customer's power plant should you expend energy.

"I'd rather have a good team working with a focused sweet spot, than a great team working with a poorly defined sweet spot".

The Sweet Spot Tool

↘ **Sweet Spot Tool**

PROFILERS	IDEAL	OFF-STRATEGY
Industry Segment		
Tendency to Adopt		
Business Discipline		
Budget		
Key Decision-Maker		
Key Customer Need		

Sweet Spot Statement

The sweet spot tool provides you with six profilers to help you consider which prospective customers are sweet spot, where your product meets their needs exactly, as well as those who are 'off-strategy' – i.e. those that in an ideal world you would prefer not to do business with.

↘ Profilers

Industry Segment

Consider a combination of propensity to buy, relative profitability (to you) & competitive landscape.
Include environmental factors – for example, regulatory compliance.

Business Discipline

Product leadership, Customer intimacy, Operational excellence.
If your product offers cost savings, customers who are focused on operational efficiency may be more suitable than ones focused on customer intimacy.

Key Decision-Maker

If your product requires a lot of behavioural change, then you need to be talking to a senior decision maker.

Tendency to Adopt

If your product is at an early stage in the market lifecycle you need a buyer prepared to take on that risk.

Budget

The budget (in financial and/or human resource terms) that a customer has for the business area to which your solution applies is a good indicator of the company's suitability as a target customer.

Key Customer Need

What is the one single requirement you want the customer to be focused on in the context of your solution? Is it process improvement? Cost savings? Convenience, etc?

Profiler 1: Industry segment

The starting point is choosing the industry sector in which to specialise. This allows you to focus on the set of prospects that are 'most likely' to purchase your product. Examples of sectors are financial services, manufacturing, technology, telecommunications, government agencies and universities. It is best to break down the sector further into market segments – for example, the financial services sector can be broken down into commercial banks, mortgage banks, retail banks and brokerage firms – each having different key requirements. They can be further broken down by size, by revenue or by number of customers.

Review market and analyst research. Evaluate barriers to entry. Familiarise yourself with the movers and shakers. Who are the big players? Who is struggling? How are the companies in this sector performing? Concentrate on segments that are growing, rather than declining. Find out whether some segments will have a more compelling reason to buy your solution than others. As with distinctive competencies in the previous chapter, get external help if you're unsure – for instance from an industry veteran with a proven track record.

Understand the strategies and strengths of existing competitors. Are they much bigger and better financed? Where are they weak? What customer segments are they targeting? What resources do they have? Who are their big customers? Which competitors are winning most of the new business (and why?) What partners can you work with to beat these competitors? (We cover this last question in Chapter 5, **Crack the Channel Code**).

Going after tightly-defined segments allows you to focus on the key problems facing a segment and to deliver superior value. Better be a mile deep and an inch wide rather than spreading your resources too thinly and being a mile wide and an inch deep, like some of your larger competitors. Become the expert or trusted advisor to the segment.

How attractive is this industry segment? How big is it? How fast is it growing? Can you win against existing competitors? How compelling is the customer need for what you have?

Ideally you or your team should have a strong background in your chosen segment. Who do you know and who knows you? Who have you sold to and delivered well to in the past?

Decide on geographic region. Should you include countries that share a common language and /or similar culture? Do you want to become a truly global player in a highly-specialised niche?

By focusing on a particular sector or segment, and selecting the geographical region, you build up a valuable body of knowledge. The know-how gained from each customer can be applied across the board. Your first customers can be used as references – with these initial 'gold' customers you can drive revenue, then through word of mouth their peers will follow. Choose a segment, dominate it and then move on.

What is the industry segment(s) you target? How many potential customers are there in this segment?

Where do the biggest opportunities lie? Is this segment of adequate size for you to compete and achieve your three year objective?

What background does your team have in your chosen segment?

What is the geographical nature of your target market? What should it be?

Who are your key competitors in that industry? How hard will it be for you to win in this sector?

Profiler 2: Tendency to adopt

Customers can be segmented by their position on the new product adoption curve. In 1991, Geoffrey Moore presented a refreshing perspective on new product adoption in his seminal book *Crossing the Chasm*. It is the market that determines whether a product is at the introductory, mainstream or mature stage. If you are at the early stages of a market lifecycle you need buyers who are prepared to take the risk involved in investing in new products. Analysing where your product sits in the market lifecycle is a good indicator when trying to find your sweet spot. In this section we will look at three stages of a market lifecycle and how they impact on your sweet spot.

Early adopters

During a new market lifecycle stage, when an innovation is introduced, customers have a steep learning curve and need lots of handholding. Certain companies are early adopters, spurred on by their awareness of the possibilities promised by a new product. Buying cycles tend to be long and customers require lots of evidence that this new innovation will solve their specific problems. At this stage of the market lifecycle your opportunity to provide real value to the customer is very high.

Pragmatists

The pragmatists will wait for the market to mature and won't be willing to take the lead until the new product has proved itself. In many cases they can see the possibilities of the solution but don't necessarily know how to apply it to their particular circumstance.

Conservatives/Sceptics

Conservatives will wait for the product to be truly mature and established before looking to purchase. Frequently, they too require help to determine how the application of the product will help their business. Finally, the sceptics will wait until everyone else has jumped on board and the product becomes commoditised – and then they're primarily concerned with price.

Adoption curve: *iPhone*

When the iPhone was launched in 2007, the average early adopters, seduced by the cool brand were educated men living in California or New York, with income greater than €75,000 per annum. As prices dropped, battery power improved and networks offered good deals, pragmatists signed up as they felt the product was proving itself. Apple is currently working on winning over the conservatives and sceptics.

The core differentiator between the three groups is their willingness to change, or more fundamentally, their awareness of the problems they have to solve, and of the potential gains. Without change, there is no opportunity for you or your competitors. If the awareness of need isn't there, the value you offer is irrelevant. If they don't think they have a problem, then from their perspective – and that's the one that counts – you don't have a solution. Figuring out where your product fits in the market lifecycle has a big impact on your choice of sweet spot. If your product belongs firmly in the 'early adopter' phase then you need a buyer who is prepared to take a risk, craves the innovation you offer and probably has a history of dealing with growing companies. If on the other hand your product fits into the 'maturity' phase, then your buyer will probably be very price conscious and this will need to be reflected in the way you present your solution.

If your product belongs firmly in the 'Early adopter' phase then you need a buyer who is prepared to take a risk, craves the innovation you offer and probably has a history of dealing with growing companies.

At what stage is the market for your product (early adopters, pragmatists, conservatives)? What evidence is there?

What other vendor products would you expect the customer to have purchased before purchasing yours?

Profiler 3: Business discipline

According to Treacy & Wiersema, authors of *The Discipline of the Market Leaders*, potential customers can be characterised by three forms of discipline that describe the way they run their businesses. You can find ways to provide value to your customers, once you have established how they conduct their business:

*   **Product leaders** break new ground in an industry, and will often be early adopters of new products;
*   **Customer intimate** companies provide excellent service to their customers for which customers are prepared to pay;
*   **Operational excellence** is at the opposite end of the scale to customer intimacy. Companies who pursue this require efficient processes and apply continuous downward pressure on costs.

Each business discipline will be interested in different solutions. So again, figure out the ideal and off-strategy business disciplines for your prospective customers.

Product Leadership

Product leaders excel at innovative product development, mobilising investment, sourcing new parts at competitive prices and creative marketing – making disproportionate noise in crowded markets, building anticipation and that magical buzz. New innovations follow rapidly to keep that product leadership position as competitors' imitations appear – think Apple Computer, Sony Corporation and Electronic Arts, the leading digital games publisher. In the food sector, think Danone, who highlight the health aspects, such as probiotics, to their product, and so appeal to a wider market and charge higher prices.

If your sweet spot customers see themselves as product leaders, your product needs to help them innovate or break new ground in their industry. They will be looking to secure a product edge over their competitors or get to market faster.

If your sweet spot customers see themselves as product leaders, your product needs to help them innovate or break new ground in their industry

Customer Intimacy

Customer intimate companies succeed by embarking on a journey with each customer. As the customer succeeds, the company succeeds. Rewards are shared and true partnerships prosper. Deep relationships mean growth within an account and referral selling to new accounts. Every customer is a reference site.

Such companies deliver tailored service and customer specific products. They exceed customers' expectations, surprise them with their level of care and take responsibility for delivering results. Successful implementation of a customer intimate business discipline means deep knowledge of customer problems and opportunities. Sales and service teams are among the most knowledgeable and best trained. Strategies are developed to fit the customer's requirements in a non-disruptive manner. Customer intimate companies become true partners with their customers.

If your sweet spot customers see themselves as customer intimate, your product needs to help them deliver better service or a new product for their customers.

Operational Excellence

In operationally excellent companies, margins are tight and the only way to make money is by volume. Growth is the only strategy and dominance of the sector is almost a pre-requisite to sustained success. Standardised operations and procedures are the key to achieving operational excellence. Such companies limit customer choice: there is no room for lots of customised products or services.

Operationally excellent companies require centralised control, since the efficiency of the company is paramount. Think low cost airlines or franchise businesses. Much of the take-up of technology in recent years has been by operationally excellent companies, driving costs out of their operations.

If your sweet spot customers are seeking operational efficiency, your solution needs to be improving their processes, helping drive down costs and increasing efficiency.

If your sweet spot customers see themselves as customer intimate, your product needs to help them deliver better service or a new product for their customers.

If your sweet spot customers are seeking operational efficiency, your solution needs to be improving their processes, helping drive down costs and increasing efficiency.

> **What is the business discipline of your sweet spot customers (product leadership, customer intimacy, or operational excellence)? What are the implications of this for you?**
>
> **What customer business disciplines are off-strategy for your company?**

Profiler 4: Budget

Some customers will have problems that they need solved and will really value your services – others will not. Beware of champagne taste and a beer budget.

Growing companies often fool themselves when it comes to evaluating how much customers should pay. Some customers will have problems that they need solved and will really value your services – others will not. Beware of champagne taste and a beer budget. Too often great products are under-priced, either because value is poorly communicated, or because the customers being pursued are off-strategy.

So how do you find out beforehand whether the customer is potentially in your sweet spot? Set an indicative range of what the total budget for your solution should be. Include upfront, ongoing and other associated costs. If you are going to invest your time and energy focusing on a market segment, adequate budgets must be available. If prospective customers are not prepared to spend the minimum amount needed to make it worthwhile for you, then you had better find another segment, or else prove your value better (see Chapter 3).

There are ways you can figure out what a customer's budget might be. For example, if they have spent €3 million on a solution, they might be prepared to spend 10–20% of that on a product that complements it. Another way is to look at sharing in the value you create for the customer. If your product saves them €1 million over a period of a year, try to capture between 10% and 20% of that figure.

Look at how your potential customers prefer to spend their money. Are they looking to spend upfront, or do they want to spread the cost over a number of years?

Use the exercise below to help figure out what the ideal budget profile should be.

What other products has the customer purchased that might impact on how yours should be priced?

Who else is selling into this sector and at what price?

What is your typical deal size? What should it be if your company is going to achieve its three year objectives?

Profiler 5: Key Decision-Maker

How are buying decisions made by your customers? Who is the key decision-maker? Who are the influencers? Is there a buying committee? Is the decision-maker a potential user of your products or services? Understand the buying process in each organisation you are targeting.

Who are your 'ideal decision makers'? For example, in a complex sale, the technology department may be involved from the outset. This sometimes entails endless cycles of meetings, as the technology buyers try to glean all the information they can in order to go and build the solution themselves. On the other hand when the decision maker is the CEO or a business line manager with an urgent problem, needing fast resolution, she will be impatient of technology geeks, and there is a much higher chance of closing the deal.

Obviously, the profile of your sweet spot decision-maker will depend on your solution but, when crafting your approach, make sure to identify the roles involved so that you can position your solution's value to meet the critical pain of the key decision makers. We will address this in the next chapter, **Creating Measurable Value**.

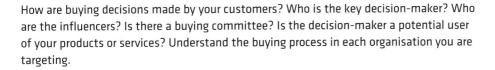

Think about your existing customers, who was the key decision maker?

Who is your ideal key decision maker?

What type of decision maker do you NOT want to be the key decision maker?

Profiler 6: Key Customer Need

What is the highest priority of your customers? Is it to innovate in their industry? Is it to release a product by a particular deadline? Is it to cut operational costs? Most industries have a number of key metrics that drive their behaviour. Learn these metrics for your sector and use these as part of your sweet spot selection criteria.

The good news is that the number of problems customers have is endless. Life in large corporations today is an endless struggle to improve, increase, transform or reduce. Your task is to determine which one of the many problems is the priority. Whether you can solve it and, above all, what value you can deliver. Here are some possibilities:

- Increase revenues
- Increase market share
- Improve operational efficiency
- Improve customer service
- Decrease operational expenses
- Speed up cash collections
- Minimise risk
- Enhance technical know-how.

We look at customer need in more depth in the next chapter, **Create Measurable Value**.

What is the single requirement that you want the customer to be focused on in the context of your type of solution?

Describe the profile of customers who have been the least profitable for you to win and service to date. Provide some sample names. Why have they been so unprofitable?

Describe the profile of customers who have been the most profitable for you to win and service to date. Provide some sample names. Why have they been so profitable?

Opportunities Outside the Sweet Spot

Opportunities outside your sweet spot will always arise. In most cases, self-discipline is required to avoid the temptation of taking on a customer that does not meet your sweet spot criteria. Time spent on a solution for an off-strategy customer robs you of time and resources better spent focusing on opportunities within your sweet spot.

A company we worked with, let's call them *Uranus*, offered a standardised solution for motor insurance underwriting. It defined its sweet spot as 'English-speaking subsidiaries of international insurers, with a typical deal size of €150,000. Head offices of international insurers are off-strategy'.

A sales opportunity arose from an international insurer to heavily customise a solution for its head office. The deal was off-strategy for two reasons: neither the market segment – 'head office' – nor the customer need – 'heavy bespoke solution' – aligned with our client's strategy. This was not a sweet spot customer. But, attracted by the prospect of a €1 million plus deal, they signed the contract.

The project took many years to complete, diverted company resources from the core business for almost a full year and nearly brought the company down. With hindsight, most of the management team would question whether it was the right decision.

However such opportunities arise in all companies. Whilst in an ideal world you should choose to say no, sometimes, usually for financial reasons, you need to say yes. Tactics we would suggest for these off-strategy deals are:

- **Evaluate the market opportunity carefully**: This could be a new sweet spot you hadn't identified;
- **Price as high as you can** and look at costs carefully, factoring in opportunity costs. Construct payment terms carefully;
- **Allocate resources carefully**: One of the difficulties with projects like these is that they tend to take up all of your senior resource – preventing growth in key areas. Outsource where you can;
- **Be honest with staff**: Explain to your team why you are taking on this deal and the scope of the project;
- **Keep very tight reins on your project management**: Bind the project scope tightly, put disciplines in place to prevent budget over-runs.

Craft Your Sweet Spot Statement

We find it useful to encapsulate your sweet spot strategy in one statement that the whole company understands. The statement should profile your ideal customers in exact terms (size, sector, budget, need) and should include what's off-strategy as a warning. It should be succinct and easy to recall. A formula that works is:

'Our sweet spot customers are... Off-strategy customer are...'

Uranus' statement from this chapter is a good example: 'our sweet spot customers are English-speaking subsidiaries of international insurers, with a typical deal size of €150,000. Head offices of international insurers are off-strategy.'

Herb Kelleher's sweet spot statement for Southwest could be: 'our sweet spot customers are price-conscious travelers, seeking to go on point-to-point journeys, who believe that "it doesn't matter what class you travel – everybody gets there at the same time". Luxury-minded travelers, looking to journey on, are off-strategy.'

The strength of the statement is that it then provides a standard reference point for the whole company – for instance engineering can explain to sales that the customer they've been asked to service are: 'outside our sweet spot'. The statement helps align everyone around the Sweet Spot Tool.

Sweet Spot Case Study
Expedia, online travel agent

We recently worked with a client – **Expedia Corporate Travel (North America)** – to help them figure out their sweet spot customer profile. Expedia provides an internet product to help corporate travel departments to book and manage travel online. The product pulls together lots of flight choices, accommodation products, and car rental options, and presents them to the traveller. Costs associated with booking the flights are a fraction of the costs incurred using a traditional travel agency. Because the product is presented as a service over the internet, it is available 24/7 and all of the trips booked for a company get aggregated to provide travel and expense management, reporting to the finance department.

Is this a solution that every company could use? Certainly any company with multiple travellers could benefit. The main benefits of Expedia's solution over traditional travel agencies are:

- 24/7 availability over the internet;
- centralised real-time reporting;
- significant cost savings.

Profiler 1 – Industry segment
We wanted to understand which industries were more likely to adopt an online solution, than retain the existing relationship with the offline travel agency. Clearly some sectors would be more comfortable with technology than others. Some would be more focused on savings, either because they operated in tight-margin sectors, or were very financially focused. These criteria pointed us towards technology companies and the manufacturing sector, because of their cost focus. Sectors that we considered off-strategy included financial services, government and non-profit organisations – we felt they would be less focused on cost savings, or more loyal to the personal service provided by traditional travel agencies.

Profiler 2 – Tendency to adopt
Expedia was introducing an innovative product and we knew that our ideal customer would have to have a buyer who fitted the profile we needed, for example keen adopters of early technology. Conversely, ideal companies might need to be red-flagged if their adoption of innovative products was below the norm. So we developed a set of questions to determine their profile and establish their 'tech-savvy-ness'. The questions included: Does the company have a widely used intranet? Does the company use the internet to do business with its customers? We felt that heavy users of technology would have a higher propensity to move their travel bookings online.

Profiler 3 – Business Discipline
One of Expedia's key benefits was a reduction in costs, so we looked to companies who

focused on operational efficiency as their primary business discipline. Again, that pointed us towards the manufacturing sector, which continually strives to drive costs out of the business. A customer intimate business discipline was off-strategy as the companies in this category would be less concerned than their more frugal counterparts about saving money.

Profiler 4 – Budget

As we explored the various deal sizes that the sales force was pursuing, we determined that the company's sweet spot was in mid-range companies. Small companies weren't worth the effort of the cost of sale. Very large companies were likely to have an infrastructure in place, including their own travel department, with executives so high up in the stratosphere that they wouldn't be inclined to book their own travel online, no matter how easy it was.

Profiler 5 – Key decision-maker

And that brought us to the decision maker criterion. If the business sponsor was identified as a senior executive in the company, then the likelihood of a deal was increased, because they were negotiating for their own activity as well as that of the rest of the travellers in the company. If, however, the decision resided within the travel department, we concluded that the required level of behaviour change was too great and that the travel managers might feel a bit like turkeys voting for Christmas.

Profiler 6 – Key customer need

And finally to the customer need. Having multiple travellers was of course a prerequisite. What did the customers really want? If they wanted to be taken care of as they travelled the world, then self-service online wouldn't be high on their agenda. If however, 24/7 access, tools in the hands of the traveller, or cost savings made their list as high priority items, then we felt that the company was a real prospect for our client.

Finally Expedia crafted its sweet spot statement:

'Our sweet spot customers are mid-range technology/manufacturing companies who are tech-savvy and travel frequently. They have an operational excellence focus and a business sponsor who is a senior executive. Financial services, government, NGOs and slow adaptors of technology are off-strategy.'

This sweet spot workshop helped Expedia improve focus and alignment amongst their management team and accelerated business growth.

↘ **Sweet spot tool,** *Expedia Corporate Travel*

● PROFILERS	● IDEAL	● OFF-STRATEGY
Industry Segment	Technology & manufacturing companies	Financial services, government, and non-profit organisations
Tendency to Adopt	Early adopters / heavy technology users	Conservatives / Slow to adopt technology
Business Discipline	Operational excellence being driven by senior executives	Customer intimacy
Budget	Mid-range company budgets	Small company budgets Large company budgets
Key Decision-Maker	Senior executive / Business sponsor	Decision maker residing in travel department
Key Customer Need	Reduce operational costs; 24/7 access, control in their hands	Companies who want 'to be taken care of'

Sweet Spot Statement

'Our sweet spot customers are mid-range technology/manufacturing companies who are tech-savvy and travel frequently. They have an operational excellence focus and a business sponsor who is a senior executive. Financial services, government, NGOs and slow adaptors of technology are off-strategy.'

Note in this example how clear the off-strategy customers are. Messaging became more focused and everybody understood the profile of the customer they were trying to serve.

Now start to build a list of your sweet spot customers, so that you can start targeting them and **creating value**, which is the subject of our next chapter.

- ↘ Introduction
- ↘ Commit to a Shared Vision
- ↘ Select your Sweet Spot Customer
- ➔ **Create Measurable Value**
- ↘ Beat the Competition
- ↘ Crack the Channel Code
- ↘ Execute The Business Battlecard™

"If you don't measure it, you probably don't care."

Tom Peters, business guru.

We worked recently with a division of a cardboard manufacturer – let's call them *Saturn*. Cardboard manufacturing is a tough business, competition is ruthless, margins are razor-thin and many regard the business as commodity hell. *Saturn* had found a sweet spot, supplying the pharmaceutical industry with packaging for transporting glass bottles to hospitals, but they weren't growing revenue or winning new customers as fast as they'd have liked. They told us: "our customers don't want to know about our product. They just keep harping on about how much we are going to make or save them."

We helped *Saturn's* CEO deepen his knowledge of the challenges facing pharmaceutical customers involved in transporting expensive products in low cost packaging. After talking to customers, we uncovered the huge losses that arise from breakage during transport, which pharmaceutical companies have to pay for. However if the goods were transported in an unbreakable box, any breakages would have to be covered by the courier. So *Saturn* developed an unbreakable box, proved the value by quoting the savings to its customers and was able to share in that value by securing a premium price.

Being able to measure and prove the value that your company creates is a cornerstone of strategy, regardless of whether you want to attract new customers or deepen relationships with existing ones.

Being able to measure and prove the value that your company creates is a cornerstone of strategy, regardless of whether you want to attract new customers or deepen relationships with existing ones.

Understanding your customers is the key to creating value, and measuring and proving that value is the key to growth.

You've now completed two parts of **the Business Battlecard** – Shared Vision and Sweet Spot. In this chapter we show how understanding your customers is the key to creating value, and how measuring and proving that value is the key to growth.

Why Create Measurable Value?

You may ask – why measure value when your customers are satisfied? You provide them with good service. They like your products, which you continually invest in. You have a good relationship with them. You even carry out regular customer satisfaction studies. So why bother measuring and proving value?

Think about the message that unquantified benefits sends to customers. In effect, you are saying "We don't care enough about you to measure how much we can impact your business". We agree with Tom Peters when he says: "If you don't measure it, you don't care."

If your company is not managing your value, you can be sure that someone else is – probably to your detriment! Is it the customers' procurement department? Or competitors, or even partners, who want to sideline you for their own advantage?

Do customers rate your value as highly as you do? How do they rate your value relative to your competitors'? When we interview customers of our client companies, there's almost always a significant difference between what our clients think their value is and what customers do. It amounts to a value gap.

Does everyone in your company understand the value being delivered? We find that in many growth companies there's a dynamic founder, who is personally an excellent spokesperson for the company, but who doesn't pass his understanding onto his team. This is a classic growth limiter. If a company's leadership is not crystal-clear about the value they offer, how can sales, marketing and production ensure that they are doing the right things? If the leadership understands the company's value, but doesn't articulate it to the team, the message is also lost.

It's been a bad decade for communicating value. The ease with which companies can use the internet to publish hyperbole about their products has created an avalanche of unwanted marketing material. Using the heavy guns of marketing to shield weak value is futile. Savvy customers aren't listening: they know the marketers are out to get them and they have their hands over their ears.

Indeed when many 'compelling value propositions' are scrutinized, their claims are not supported and they are little more than hype and puffery. But marketers gets a bad rap – if the company doesn't make it clear exactly what it wants them to communicate, how can their job be any different to 'putting lipstick on the pig'? Unfortunately our marketers don't know what they don't know and are left with only hyperbole to cover the cracks.

Embellishing the credentials of offerings is a time-honoured practice. Unsubstantiated claims are made and sales people are given license to exaggerate. Experienced buyers are on to this game. Despite this, many companies continue in such flawed practices. Is there a better way? Sure there is.

When thinking about the value you create for your customers, think in terms of measurable value. Buyers have no time for unsubstantiated declarations of value. Can you answer and back up the question 'How much do you make or save me?' If not, you are not measuring or proving your value. Understanding how to create, deliver and prove value can turn small companies into large ones and large ones into giants.

In this chapter, we outline an approach to help you create and prove measurable value:
* **Who** you need to convince: identify the key **buying influencers**;
* Understand the **pain or problem** facing your customers, and create value which alleviates that pain;
* **Measure** the value you are promising to deliver;
* Provide objective **proof** or **evidence** of the value you delivered;
* **State** your value.

Understanding how to create, deliver and prove value can turn small companies into large ones and large ones into giants.

Create Measurable Value Tool

↘ Create Measurable Value Tool

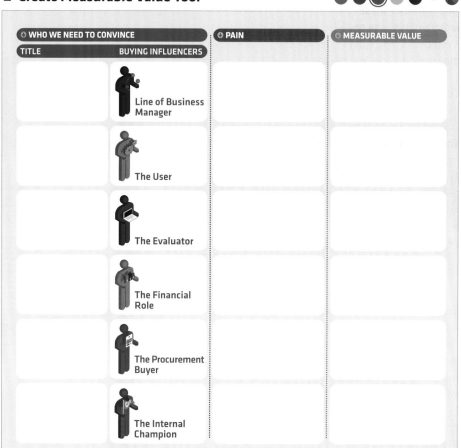

Measurable Value Statement

Buying Influencers

In business to business selling, there are a number of people you have to convince of your value. We call these 'buying influencers'. Each buying influencer has his or her own requirements, risk profiles, and agenda. We have identified six generic buying influencers - you can supply specific names and titles for your own circumstances. The same person may perform one or more roles during the buying process.

The roles are:

Line of Business Manager

The opportunity usually starts here. Depending on the size of the company, the line of business manager is usually a vice president, general manager or director of a main department. Typically, they have functional responsibility for an area of the business, control over a pre-approved budget, and are concerned with solving a particular business problem. This role is central. Uncovering the impact of key problems on the line of business manager is essential. You can be sure she is always going to be concerned about how much you're going to make and save the company.

The User

The user is concerned with the day-to-day operational issues of using your product. For instance, if your product were aimed at accounting, the user would be the person doing the daily accounting, rather than financial control. A user can rarely make a deal happen but, almost certainly, can stop it. Users will need to be convinced that training, documentation, reliability, and service are satisfactory. The value they care about is time – how much time will this product save them and how will it help them achieve targets?

The Evaluator

The evaluator will more than likely have a technical focus. He wants to know how your solution will fit with existing in-house products, standards and expertise. Often he has a bias against bought-in solutions, and will seek hard evidence that your product works. He has the ability to say 'no' to any proposed solution.

The Financial Role

The financial buyer will generally be the CFO, whose focus is almost always the bottom line. They always seek measurable value. The key question is always return on investment or 'If I spend a dollar, how much will I make or save?' Their role is to green light or veto a project. Generally they don't get involved in the technical terms of the deal but will look for savings on your price – so make sure you budget for some!

The Procurement Buyer

Depending on the company, the procurement officer may co-ordinate the entire buying cycle. Service level agreements, penalty clauses, payment terms, warranty and maintenance, and confidentiality and trade secrets are all items to be negotiated. Procurement is concerned with risk and price. Their job is to get price concessions, and to negotiate water-tight contracts.

The Internal Champion

Frequently one of the other roles will double up as a champion. The evaluator may be a real fan of your product. The line of business manager might value your industry expertise, or the financial buyer, could be a supporter, because you have demonstrated cost savings in the past. Without someone on the inside to communicate your value in your absence, it will be difficult to make your measurable value stick.

Start thinking about your own customers – can you identify some or all of the roles we have outlined?

Typically who are the key buying influencers that you deal with?

What generic buying influencer title – Line of Business, Evaluator etc. – would you assign to each person?

Rank each of the buying influencers in order of their importance.

Understand Your Customers' Pain

The talent at the reins of many growing companies have a product and service focus. And rightly so! Their insights continually create exciting innovations. But too often products are designed for the engineers who create them rather than the customers who use them. Sure, it's easier and more fun for engineers (or sales people) to talk about a product's great features, but customers don't buy your product, they buy what your product will do for them. As Harvard marketing professor Theodore Levitt told his MBA students:

> *"People don't want to buy a quarter-inch drill. They want a quarter-inch hole."*

Focus on the customer's needs, not on the features of your solution. If you want to create value, start to understand your customers' needs better than anybody else. Obviously customers have multiple needs and you can't, and don't have to, solve all of them. Your job is to identify which customer needs take priority - in other words what's causing unbearable pain.

Your job is to identify which customer needs take priority – in other words what's causing pain.

Understand how each customer prioritises – is price more important than quality, service more important than advanced features? Devote time to bridging the gap between what your product offers and what customers really need.

Getting the job done now: *IKEA*

Furniture retailer IKEA provides a good example from the consumer world of how understanding customer needs is key to growth. In furniture retailing, stores were traditionally positioned according to quality, price and depth of product range. Given the risks for retailers in investing in furniture inventory, customers often had to wait two or three months before getting their longed-for items.

IKEA discovered that for young people in starter homes 'getting the job done now' was of primary importance. The 'unbearable pain' for these customers was waiting three months for delivery in unfurnished apartments, where they had nowhere to sleep or eat.

The road to understanding what customers value has to start with the customer. Yet feature-focused presentations, supported by 'death by PowerPoint' and delivered with the rat-a-tat-tat of an Uzi sub-machine gun persist. They just confuse and turn away potential customers.

Put yourself in the position of the senior executives. Set aside the feature machine gun. Realise that what's uppermost in their minds is getting products to market faster, improving customer retention, beating competitors, reducing costs or growing revenue. In simple terms, they want to get jobs done.

The customer's evaluation team may be interested in your cool product or in seeing how it works. But the heads of department will only give you their undivided attention if you are addressing their priority problems.

Help your team to understand customers' needs. Get them on the value discovery trail. Time spent in reconnaissance is seldom wasted. Those working closest to the customer often provide the best insights. Don't wait for customer queries or complaints to arrive. Become a trusted advisor.

Time spent in reconnaissance is seldom wasted.

At one of our strategy workshops a participant, whose company provides chemical solutions for manufacturing, stated that her company's aim was to 'understand the customer more profoundly than they understand themselves'. She showed how they achieve this:

> "Usually we have a first meeting with the production manager to discuss issues. However, to get to the nub of the issue, it is often necessary to talk to those at the coal-face. So, we ask for an introduction to the production line supervisors. We talk to them, and offer to come back at the end of the shift when they are less busy.

> "This has a two-fold result – firstly, the production line supervisors are delighted that someone had acknowledged that mid-production is a busy period and is taking enough interest to come back when they have more time. Secondly, the production manager is generally not around at that stage, so we get to have more open conversations with the guys at the coal-face – giving us insight into latent problems and unarticulated pain."

Find a way to communicate with as many of your customer's buying influencers as possible. The key to understanding their pain is to ask good questions. Don't make assumptions about the problem. Once you have identified an area of concern, get to the root of it. Who is impacted? What is the impact? How have they tried to resolve this issue? What worked, what didn't? Do they have any idea what costs might be involved?

For many industries, there are published benchmarks. Study these and find out how your customer rates in relation to their peers. Get help from an industry veteran to understand the key metrics driving revenues and costs. Such experts often have a broad range of contacts, credibility with key customers, and can provide valuable insights. Hire people who have worked for customers trying to solve similar problems.

Create value

One of our clients, let's call them *Perseus*, is a growing company specialising in the design of integrated circuit chips. Their approach to selling was to produce a list of benefits they thought their product provided to their customers.

Many of these claimed benefits were irrelevant to their customers. *Perseus* had simply adopted a 'spray and pray' approach to communicating their value. Because of this they were getting limited sales.

Perseus had simply adopted a 'spray and pray' approach to communicating their value. Because of this they were getting limited sales.

We spent time with *Perseus'* customers. Here are some of the questions we asked:

- What is the critical issue you're trying to resolve?
- How many days per month are spent trying to resolve this issue?
- How many staff are affected when this system does not work?
- How many times do these breakdowns happen per year?
- What is the cost for those involved?
- What is the annual cost?
- What was the overall business impact?

Finally we held a focus group with the buying influencers, where we explained our understanding of their pain and asked for feedback.

Perseus now had an in-depth understanding of their customers' pain and knew where to create value. They tweaked their product so that it addressed customer needs, and also removed irrelevant features. They made sure that they created value for each buying influencer – for instance, they increased their post-purchase support to satisfy the user, and budgeted in savings to meet the financial buyer's needs.

Once you've understood the pain being experienced by each of the customer's buying influencers, you're in a position to create value for them by fixing that pain.

Put yourself in the customers' shoes. Consider each major feature and benefit of your product or service and keep asking 'so what?' Repeat the question until you understand exactly what value is provided to each of your customer's buying influencers. Continuously challenge your assumptions. Once you understand how you are creating value, you will know where to invest resources.

Look at ways to tweak your product, build services around it, and broaden your offering.

Remember the customer has multiple projects to choose from. If the value you create is not significant enough to get you on the radar, then possibly you need to look at other opportunities.

Describe the situation for your customers before they buy your product.

How do they typically manage to solve the problem if they are not using your product?

What is the impact of this problem on the customer's business? Who does it impact?

What is the key pain or need of each of your buying influencers?

Measure it!

When asked to explain the value they provide, too many vendors sound like copywriters under duress. As one senior executive put it to us:

"Why do so many vendors lie? They tell us they are the fastest and most comprehensive and all that jargon. We know it is not true. We spend thousands of dollars with analysts to keep us up to speed. With all this gobbledygook, vendors break their promises, before we even start to engage. Give me a vendor any day that talks in my language, can help me fix my problems and keeps their promises."

Describing products in vague terms that are not measurable is depressingly prevalent – and always unhelpful. Airily telling buyers that your solution will reduce their costs, without actually measuring what those costs are, looks half-hearted, lazy and opportunistic. Do the work and run the numbers to turn a perceived vague value into a real measurable one.

When customers think about measuring value, they are weighing up questions like:

* **How much** will I save or make by adopting this solution?
* **How long** will it be before I will see a return?
* **What** are the **risks** (to me personally in terms of career and to my company) that this project will fail and I will not see any return?
* **What resources** will I have to invest in this project to make it happen?
* **What** is this going to **cost** me?
* **How important** is this project relative to the other pressing projects that I am considering?

No longer is it good enough to trot off a set of generic answers to these questions. Buyers have had enough of vague promises. They want to know exactly how much you will save them, what concrete risks are involved, and how you plan to address those risks.

Analysts IDC carried out research that shows that an investment of $1m typically has a decision cycle of 18 months. However, once a customer can measure the impact, 65% of purchases occur in six months or less. Being able to prove to customers the amount, and the timeframe in which you can reduce their key costs, increase revenue growth or achieve market share objectives will set you apart from the competition.

If you don't know the measurable value you create, then how do you know how much to charge? Are you charging too much? Too little? In our experience growing companies often undercharge because they're desperate for business and don't understand the true value they're providing. Before they know it they're in a downward spiral. If you want to grow your business, build a repeatable process for measuring the value you create.

If you want to grow your business, build a repeatable process for measuring the value which you create.

Substantiate your claims by showing that you have the people, processes, tools and experience necessary to deliver the value that you've promised. Get input from the buying influencers to underpin your business case. This can help create a shared sense of ownership.

As your customer decides to make an investment, help him determine what return he will get. For every dollar spent, there must be more than a dollar returned. That return can be measured, in tangible benefits such as reduced cost of production, increased sales, reduced operating costs etc. There may also be more intangible benefits such as great user satisfaction with your product – if the customer has had a great experience using your product he will want to blow your trumpet at speaking slots and to industry analysts. We cover how to capture this customer satisfaction in the section below, 'Prove your value'.

Building measurable pilot projects

Many growing companies offer a 'try before you buy' pilot approach to allow the customer assess potential value before purchase. But too many of these pilots don't measure value.

A client of ours had more pilots than British Airways. This company, let's call them *Ceres*, offered customers the opportunity to pilot their product to prove that the technology worked (which it did). *Ceres* was an early stage company with a limited customer base. Despite the fact that the pilots proved technically successful they weren't converting to purchase orders. The user buyers and evaluators loved their solution but the financial buyers and line of business managers still needed to be convinced.

Working with *Ceres*, we built a 'value calculator' that compared process efficiency before and after their solution was implemented.

We chose one of *Ceres'* more enthusiastic prospective customers' and looked at the critical customer activities where the solution would have a positive impact such as cost of sales, product rework, customer retention, productivity and capital expenditure. We made some assumptions jointly with the customer, and did a 'before and after' test.

Our 'value calculator' identified real cost savings based on customer operations and made an unequivocal business case, jointly created with the customer. Ceres was able to stand over its promise to 'reduce the number of man hours by 20% and deliver a saving of $500,000 in the first year'. The ability to demonstrate their measurable value finally convinced the sceptical financial buyers to buy.

Ceres had now an easy-to-use value calculator that they insisted on incorporating in every future pilot. They built a library of results so they could fine-tune their assumptions and be confident about promising savings, based on experience with several customer implementations.

If you use pilot projects, think about incorporating a value calculator, which your sales team find easy to use and which demonstrates before and after revenue increases and savings. Remember – unquantified value will go unrewarded.

Remember – unquantified value will go unrewarded.

> **What measurable value does your product deliver? Do you know? Do your customers know?**
>
> **Describe the situation after your customers buy your product.**
>
> **How would you go about assessing the value your product creates?**
>
> **Think of a successful project – how much did this project save your customer? Grow revenue for your customer?**

Prove it!

So far we've looked at diagnosing customer needs, creating value and measuring it by, for instance, pilot projects and value calculators. Measuring value pre-purchase helps win sales from a few customers. But proving value post-purchase ensures winning lots more sales from lots more customers.

Many buyers of innovative offerings are still suffering from buyer's remorse. Promises made in long forgotten sales proposals continue to haunt them. Their risk index is high; they want to see tangible proof before signing another purchase order.

The true sales opportunity exists post-purchase – understand the ways you created value and you will have a treasure trove of information to reassure existing customers and attract new ones.

Moment of Proof

As the customer installation project nears completion, everyone's exhausted; they're ready to move on, already thinking of the next big thing. The last thing anyone wants is take stock, write a review and go through the numbers. In any case your product worked, the customer's happy, so why bother? Unfortunately when things go well people have short memories – although they'll remember mishaps forever – so your customer may soon forget the value you delivered.

The project isn't over until you've proved your value. Your final task is to quantify post-purchase the value you delivered, and get the customer's sign-off. There's a moment when this should be done – the honeymoon period, when the customer is seeing the first really positive results of your product and is delighted at the value you've delivered. We call this the 'moment of proof' and it needs to be seized. Leave it even a week and the goodwill may have evaporated.

The project isn't over until you've proved your value. Your final task is to quantify post-purchase the value you delivered, and get the customer's sign-off.

Document and disseminate your story

Get the value you have delivered for your customers documented in well-crafted case studies. Handpick customers that others will be interested in reading about. Make heroes out of your customers' employees. Get them speaking slots to talk about their success with you. Customers that recommend your product to their peers – not because they're getting a deal from you, but because they genuinely love your product and your people - are gold customers and should be treated as such.

By articulating your value in well-written and well-publicised case studies, you shift the focus from trying to sell a product to posing the question: *'Would you like to achieve the value of between $x and $y, provided by our product, in z timeframe, as our existing clients have?'*

Make industry experts your advocates

When evaluating key purchases, customers are heavily swayed by industry experts, including analysts, who provide important reassurance of suppliers' claims. Smart buyers seek independent opinions, particularly if the solution being reviewed is innovative.

Treat relationships with industry experts as you would a key strategic account.

Treat relationships with industry experts as you would a key strategic account. Keep in regular contact. Give them information you come across that may be useful to them. Give opinion – even contrary opinion – on movements in the marketplace. Share your competitive analysis with them and seek their insights and views.

A number of years ago a client of ours, Steeltrace, who provided a software development tool, experienced just how critical relationships with analysts can be:

> "We were in the process of signing our first big US customer, when our CEO received a phone call. Our customer had strict procurement policies and one of their rules was a rating by a particular analyst. We were advised that, if we could sort this problem out, the deal could proceed. So, our choice was to build a relationship with the analyst, or to walk away from the deal. We contacted a source within the analyst firm and began discussions to rectify the situation. The analyst understood the measurable value Steeltrace delivered and communicated that to the customer. The deal was signed."

What proof or evidence do you have of your measurable value?

Who could provide it?

What relationships do you have with industry experts? How should you improve them?

What customer case studies, or independent expert reports should you consider getting commissioned?

State Your Value

Finally, **state your value** in succinct, measurable phrases. Come up with different statements for each buying influencer. For instance for a financial controller looking at a new customer relationship management system, the measurable value statement might be:

'We will help you grow your business by between X% and Y% in timeframe Z.'

Alternatively, a value statement focused at a production manager might be:

'Our solution will decrease processing time by 10% within three months, freeing you up for other tasks.'

When you've gone through the different buying influencers, try to express your measurable value in one statement. The statement should be as clear and brief as possible. *Ceres'* value statement mentioned earlier in the chapter is a good one: 'reduce the number of man hours by 20% and deliver a saving of $500,000 in the first year'. It's short, to the point, and measurable, with an in-built deadline.

Create Measurable Value Case Study
Jupiter, Lighting solutions

A client of ours, *Jupiter*, is a growing company which provides innovative lighting solutions for engineering companies. Their product saved clients lots of money but they were finding it hard to close deals. *Jupiter's* larger competitors were incumbent suppliers and they were not slow about pointing out the risks of *Jupiter's* innovative lighting solutions. *Jupiter's* sweet spot criteria included high energy users, and early adopters of new products, who had senior level people with budgets to drive green initiatives. Within their sweet spot, they needed to convince multiple buying influencers, concerned with costs and green issues.

We worked with *Jupiter* to build a picture of the people they would need to convince of the value of their offering.

Line of Business Manager / Financial role
General managers and financial buying influencers were mainly concerned with cost savings and needed hard evidence. These were the key people *Jupiter* needed to convince.

Jupiter quickly discovered that they had to be able to demonstrate measurable value if senior managers were to be convinced. They encouraged the senior managers to go with a small pilot initially and measure the 'before and after' installation energy cost savings. They used this process to produce a generic spreadsheet, which allowed each new engineering customer put in their own assumptions, to validate whether promised cost savings would be realized. Over time this exercise allowed Jupiter to stand over their guarantee of a 40–50% reduction in costs.

Users – Factory Floor Supervisor
Senior people on the factory floor were concerned with downtime due to poor lighting, so *Jupiter* was able to demonstrate that their lights would save 5% on employee downtime.

Evaluators – Safety Managers/HR
HR were concerned with possible litigation costs due to outdated lighting systems, causing eyestrain. Safety managers wanted everything to pass the appropriate regulations. *Jupiter* had to provide reassurances that their lighting would result in a litigation-free environment.

Legal/Procurement
Procurement were concerned with risk. What if Jupiter went bust? What were the project risks? *Jupiter* used reputable local partners to help reduce any perceived risk.

Internal Champions – Energy managers
Many of the energy managers were keen to meet green targets and championed the solution, but they had limited influence to make anything happen.

Measurable Value Tool – *Jupiter, Lighting Solutions*

WHO WE NEED TO CONVINCE		⏱ PAIN	⏱ MEASURABLE VALUE
TITLE	**BUYING INFLUENCERS**		
General Manager	Line of Business Manager	Cut energy costs.	Reduce lighting energy consumption by 40-50% within 12 months
Factory Floor supervisor	The User	Downtime due to outdated lighting	Saving on employee downtime by 5%
HR/ safety manager	The Evaluator	Outdated lighting systems giving rise to eye strain	Better quality lighting offering litigation-free environment
CFO	The Financial Role	Reduce operating costs	Reduced operating costs
Procurement	The Procurement Buyer	Minimise risk and reduce litigation costs	Personal goals of meeting green initiative targets
Energy Manager	The Internal Champion	Address green initiatives targets	Meet green targets

Measurable Value Statement

Our green compliant solution will reduce energy costs by 40-50% within a year, reduce litigation costs, guarantee quality lighting, save employee downtime by 5%, and help meet green initiative targets.

Creating, measuring and proving your value to customers is essentially a cooperative process. Beating the competition is essentially a competitive one, and we address this in the next chapter, **Beat the Competition**.

- ↘ **Introduction**
- ↘ **Commit to a Shared Vision**
- ↘ **Select your Sweet Spot Customer**
- ↘ **Create Measurable Value**
- ⊙ **Beat the Competition**
- ↘ **Crack the Channel Code**
- ↘ **Execute The Business Battlecard™**

"The first sign of madness is doing the same things over and over again and expecting a different result."

Albert Einstein.

In the late 1990s, Mark Benioff's Salesforce.com entered the market with a vision to create a web based customer relationship management service that would beat the traditional technology competitors. Rather than long and expensive implementations, Salesforce.com offered an on-demand service that could be accessed over the internet.

Salesforce.com created a whole new way to deliver automated sales, marketing and support operations. It tackled the competition head-on, delivering a web-based solution based on subscription payment with no up-front licensing fee. By eliminating expensive set-up, maintenance and upgrade costs, Benioff effectively took the risk factor out of the equation. Salesforce.com's 'no pain' adoption approach was in stark contrast to the long implementation cycles being offered by competitors.

By changing the rules of the game, Salesforce.com beat many larger competitors. In the last chapter we looked at the importance of creating measurable value. In this chapter we examine the question – **why should a customer buy from you rather than the competition?**

We often ask growing companies how they differ from the competition. Sometimes it is like talking to an alcoholic in denial – deep down they know they should be doing something about it, but it never gets the true attention it needs until there is a crisis. Being able to beat the competition lies at the heart of your strategy. It is about creating and sustaining superior value based on a set of unique activities, which your customers really value. Creating a strategy that beats the competition is not simply a sales or marketing question – it is a central strategic issue, located firmly at the door of your company's leadership team.

It is about creating and sustaining superior value based on a set of unique activities, which your sweet spot customers really value.

Recognise that, for any business customer, there are inevitable risks involved in buying from a growing company. So why would any business customer consider buying from you, unless you can offer value that is superior to incumbent suppliers?

Focus on delivering superior value for your customers – or else you are on the road to commoditisation. Great companies do things for their customers that their rivals either cannot or will not do. If you perform the same activities in the same way as your competitors, you can only be differentiated on one thing – price. There can only be a few winners at the price game so don't be surprised if the results aren't what you had hoped for.

If you perform the same activities in the same way as your competitors, you can only be differentiated on one thing – price.

Beating the competition has become harder. You used to be able to set a direction for your business, craft your strategy and execute it. But now the timescales are shorter. Your value proposition is easily copied by competitors, many of whom will undercut you on price.

As in previous chapters, beating the competition involves a trade-off in choices. You cannot be all things to all customers. The way you choose to beat the competition will depend on your shared vision, your selected sweet spot customers and the value you deliver. Your **Business Battlecard** will reflect this alignment.

For instance take two examples from the food service sector. Michelin restaurants concentrate on wealthy and aspiring customers; they beat the competition on the quality of their ingredients, their cooking, and the service. They seek to deliver a 'superior cuisine, worth a special journey'. Starbucks doesn't differentiate on quality of ingredients – their coffee is not significantly better than competitors. Instead they beat the competition on ambience. Customers flock to Starbucks for the comfortable leather seating, the restrained music and the customer experience referred to as the 'third place', a communal meeting place between work and home. Starbucks have been able to capture that value by charging over $4 for a cup of latte.

In this chapter, we will help you beat the competition in a systemic way through a set of repeatable steps:

- Understand how your **industry competes**;
- **What do you do differently?**
- **ROLE reversal**: Review your key company activities and assess whether they should be **Reduced**, **Omitted** or **Outsourced**, **Left unchanged**, or **Enhanced**;
- Craft a **'beat the competition'** statement.

Beat The Competition Tool

↘ **Beat The Competition Tool** ● ● ● ◐ ● = ◔

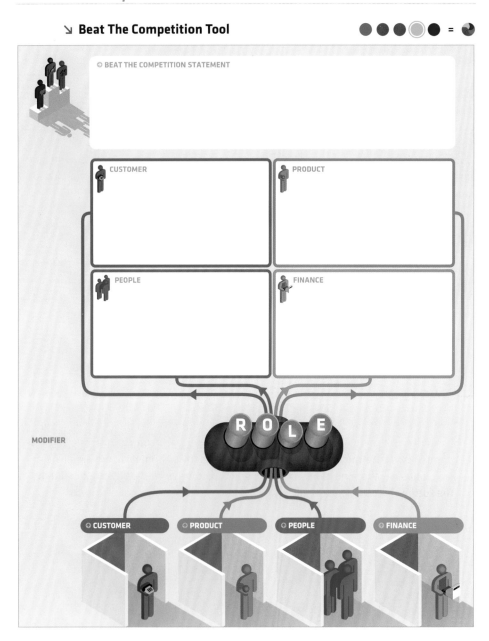

○ BEAT THE COMPETITION STATEMENT

CUSTOMER

PRODUCT

PEOPLE

FINANCE

R O L E

MODIFIER

○ CUSTOMER　○ PRODUCT　○ PEOPLE　○ FINANCE

Modifier options

 R Reduce　 **O** Omit or Outsource　 **L** Leave　 **E** Enhance

The 'Beat the Competition' tool helps you explore how to do things differently, and where you are going to allocate scarce resources. When looking at your company activities, repeatedly consider the phrase: *'unlike our competitors, we...'* This will form the basis of your Beat the Competition statement.

Understand How Your Industry Competes

How did Salesforce.com figure out how to beat the competition? By understanding how its industry competed.

Through in-depth understanding of its industry's competitive terrain, Salesforce gained insight into customers' frustration with long lead times, and broke its industry's shared belief in how software is delivered.

Be like Salesforce. Immerse yourself in your industry, review published materials, look at your competitors' practices, talk to industry experts – and of course potential customers – to find out what really counts in your industry. Only when you know what really counts, can you work out how you're going to do things differently to deliver superior value. Look at the company which does things best in your sector. Dissect the reasons for their success. What can you learn from them?

In our strategy work with clients, we use some of the following exploratory questions to help them figure out ways to beat the competition. Try some of them for your own sector:

Industry standards: What are the shared beliefs or accepted ways of doing business in your industry? Are these beliefs still in the best interest of the customer? Are there any emerging trends that make these beliefs less sound? What do trends in other industries tell us about how your sector will change? Are incumbents acting on these trends? What are the things that frustrate and annoy customers about suppliers in your industry? What government and regulatory issues will impact on your industry in the future?

Customer insights: Which customers are being offered products that are too broad and functionally rich for their needs? Which are outsourcing current work because they can't do it internally as nobody has offered them a simple, easy-to-use solution?

Which are frustrated with the limitations of existing products and would pay more for better, more rounded products? What unarticulated customer needs can you find through 'living a day' with your customers? How do you bring the voice of the customer into your company?

Do the existing roles of 'who does what' in your industry make sense? Is there a way of making it easy for customers to perform tasks you normally perform, and provide them with superior value and savings?

Value capture: How are products priced in your sector? Per day or per project? By one-off payments or recurring payments? How much do partners contribute to and get from each deal? How price-sensitive are customers? How is the internet changing the sales, marketing and delivery processes for your industry? What way can it reduce costs for you and provide greater value for your customers?

Growth Model: How can you leverage your time with customers so that you acquire knowledge to build new competencies, and so that you get paid for what you know, rather than what you do? How can you find ways for customers to fund your research and development? How can you build customer and partner information into a repeatable delivery package?

Transforming higher education: *University of Phoenix*

The University of Phoenix, founded 1976, understood how its industry competed and crafted a new approach to education. Their insight was that adult learners wanting to advance their careers while working were not well served by traditional universities.

Whilst the traditional universities churned out graduates from pristine campuses, which offered social and sporting activities to complement academic pursuits, the University of Phoenix saw that there was a market for adult learners (applicants over 23) who wanted to follow targeted accredited programmes, whilst continuing to work.

Phoenix started off by renting space, rather than building traditional campuses. Adult students attend highly focussed classes, complemented today by state of the art eLearning. Many of the conveniences that 21st century students take for granted were pioneered by the University of Phoenix: online classes and delivery, continuous enrolment, computer simulations. This 30-year old 'upstart' institution is now the largest private university in North America with two hundred campuses, over 300,000 students and revenue close to $3 billion in 2007.

Seek evidence to test the insights you get. Prioritise and discuss them with colleagues and people you trust. They will help you in the next step, which is figuring out how to do things differently, so that you can pull ahead of the competition.

What are the shared beliefs in your industry? Are these beliefs still in the best interests of the customer? What can you learn from how other industries develop?

What customer insights should you seek? How should you try to get them?

What competencies have you got that you can leverage?

Can the existing ways of value capture (pricing) be changed in your industry?

What do you do differently?

In 2002 Virgin Mobile entered the US cellular services market, which was highly competitive and dominated by major players. But by doing away with long term contracts, focusing on consumers under 30, offering stylish phones, entertainment features, simplified pricing, and their famously irreverent brand, Virgin carved out a niche.

Virgin didn't take on the big players on their own terms – it used Sprint's network and didn't go after corporate business customers. It found the gap – in this case the young, cost-conscious and style-conscious – and targeted them aggressively using a prepaid only approach. Within five years of entering the US market, Virgin had acquired over 5 million customers, was close to breaking even and on a trajectory to achieve revenues of over a $1 billion in 2008.

Virgin drew its own road map – which is more fun than following the leader. Doing things differently means freeing yourself from convention. If you just follow the tried and tested paths, you are unlikely to break new ground.

When you examine your industry, you'll find that there are always well-established, better-funded competitors, who have secured lots of customers, and built deep partnerships. The good news is that these apparent strengths can also be weaknesses. These large Goliaths are slow and ponderous. Their mindset, internal processes and entrenched market position make it hard for them to change. Opportunities that you would seize often have little interest for them, as they are only interested in opportunities that add millions of dollars in revenue.

The implications for growing companies are clear. Look to obtain a fresh view on your industry. Become a contrarian. Force competitors to compete by new rules. Find new partners. Deliver new value. Invest in areas where competitors are weak. You are probably more customer-centric and entrepreneurial than your larger competitors, with their specialised silos. You have a better chance of understanding and developing a rounded view of unmet and unarticulated customer needs.

Look to obtain a fresh view on your industry. Become a contrarian. Force competitors to compete by new rules.

Examine the key activities within your company in terms of the value each delivers to the customer. Think about how the combined activities could create superior value to help you beat the competition. Only companies that are obsessive about creating value which is hard for competitors to copy continue to win.

Remember the **distinctive competencies**, which you considered in Chapter 1, **Commit to a Shared Vision**? Now think about applying those competencies to beating the competition.

Your main differentiator – or your superior value – should be based on your distinctive competencies. Try to leverage areas where you have proved competence to beat the competition and make it difficult for rivals to emulate.

Taking over the high street: *Zara*

Zara, the Spanish retail chain replaced 'high fashion' with 'fast fashion' when it arrived on the UK high streets in 1999. Traditionally, retailers offered three or four seasons but Zara offered new flirty stock every week, and this caught UK stores on the hop.

How did Zara trump competitors by getting new designs to stores so quickly, efficiently and cheaply? Unlike traditional retailers, who outsource their clothes manufacturing to Asia, most of Zara's manufacturing is in Europe, principally in Spain. They have a computer-based production and distribution system that enables them to get from drawing board to shop floor within 10 days. Unlike their rivals who had central design teams, Zara assigned young design teams to each category – one for women's wear, one for men's and one for children.

Unlike their rivals, if a shop in the high street ran out of an item, the manager could order more or suggest alterations onto his shop computer allowing the designers to see the request instantaneously. Zara spent almost nothing on advertising, rather than the industry traditional 4% of turnover – instead their rapidly changing window displays in flagship stores fuelled word of mouth. Finally, their determinedly low prices lured the consumer and enabled fast stock turnover.

Zara's insight was to replace high fashion with time-based or 'fast fashion'. Through creating a self-reinforcing set of activities different to the competition's, they delivered on this insight. Zara brought cost-effective catwalk interpretations quickly onto the high street, spawning a plethora of imitators – such as Top Shop, Oasis, Miss Selfridges – and alarming the luxury brands.

When thinking about differentiation, ask yourself – and your customers – the simple question: 'What do we do that's different from the competition?' Differentiation is only successful if you can be better at something that your customers value. Just being different doesn't mean you're delivering superior value. There is no point building advantages that no-one wants.

Doing things differently doesn't necessarily mean starting a revolution. Be realistic. If you're Google, you can afford to be highly disruptive, but for most growing companies, doing things differently means tweaking, amending, and subtly changing. You're looking for an edge, not reinventing the wheel.

Sometimes doing things differently means learning from a role model in another sector or another jurisdiction. Michael O'Leary didn't have an original insight for Ryanair, but he made an exhaustive study of Southwest Airlines. His insight was adopting the American 'no frills/low fare' mindset to Europe.

What are the top three areas in which you could differentiate from your competition?

How might you test whether customers value these differences?

How would you get the resources to profitably execute on these differences?

Are these potential differentiators defensible? How easy is it for competitors to match them?

Differentiation is only successful if you can be better at something that your customers value.

ROLE Reversal

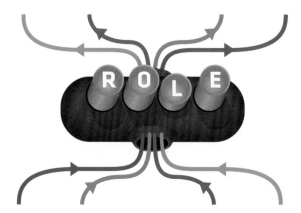

You have looked closely at how your industry competes and you've started developing insight into how to do things differently. Now it's time to deliver on this insight by refining your company's activities.

Insight is meaningless without action. Zara's insight on how to do things differently was 'fast fashion' rather than high fashion, but it was the way Zara adjusted activities to deliver on this insight that enabled them to beat the competition.

Regardless of whether you're making a radical move or a more incremental change, you can look at refining your company activities using what we call the 'ROLE' model.

ROLE is an acronym for Reduce, Omit or Outsource, Leave, Enhance. When you ROLE through your company, you scrutinize each activity and decide what adjustment it needs.

To clarify this process, we generally start with the four key company areas that we defined in Chapter 1 – Customer, Product, People, Financial – and we look at the activities carried out in each of these areas to assess whether they should be **reduced**, **omitted** or **outsourced**, **left** unchanged or **enhanced**.

After a rigorous 'ROLE through', company activities are honed and improved. Those areas where more value could be added are enhanced, those that are wasteful and inefficient are reduced or omitted entirely, and those that are already working well are left alone on the principle of 'if it ain't broke, don't fix it'. ROLE-ing through brings clarity and discipline to the process of streamlining your company

Remember how the University of Phoenix **reduced** their customers to 'working adults over

23' and **reduced** class time; **omitted** large palatial central campuses; **left** accreditation **unchanged**; but **enhanced** online delivery though pioneering technology and internet usage, and **enhanced** payment options. They translated their original insight into a set of activities to win.

In seeking to beat the competition, many companies focus their energy only on their products or services. But you have the opportunity to differentiate from the moment customers decide they need a new solution, to the time when they decide to dispose of it. The advantage of ROLE-ing through the four functional areas is that it forces you to look at people, customers, and financial issues, not just product.

ROLE-ing through the iPOD

Steve Jobs (Apple CEO) launched the iPOD with the shared vision of '1000 songs in your pocket' at the height of the digital music rush in 2001. Apple's insight was driven partly by the need to increase iMac sales and partly by a desire to capitalise on music lovers who were trading their songs like crazy on Napster (an online illegal music sharing service).

Nobody had yet found the recipe for the digital music market and there was no clear market leader. Let's ROLE through the Apple iPOD product building process:

Reduce: Reduce the number of features and make it as easy to use as possible. Reduce the product to the size of a pack of cards and the price per song to $1.

Outsource or Omit: Outsource the drive from Toshiba, a battery from Sony, chips from Texas Instruments and Portal Player and software from Pixo.

Leave: Leave other Apple Engineering features as they are, but ensure the technology is suitable for the miniature iPod.

Enhance: Enhance the music experience by making it easy to transfer songs and make it work seamlessly with iTunes. Enhance design to look and feel great, from the excellence of the Apple detail to getting the wheel to turn faster as the menu gets longer.

Prêt à Manger's recipe for success

Prêt à Manger is a good example of a company, which successfully practised ROLE reversal. In an industry, which offers bland, sometimes unhealthy products, miserable employees and which celebrates conformity, Prêt à Manger managed to rewrite the rule book by ROLE-ing through their company activities.

Customer

They **omitted** customers who wanted a sit-down meal but enhanced their focus on customers who were time-pressed and health-conscious.

They **enhanced** the company image, launching themselves as a green, employee-friendly company. To make good their promise to 'contribute to a cleaner, greener and altogether more sustainable society', they give away food that is not used within the day to local charities and homeless people.

Product

They **omitted** seating, which meant no waiters or waitresses, less cleaning-up for staff and faster turn-around time. They left the concept of fast food alone – in fact the average customer is in and out with their food in about 90 seconds – probably faster than your local McDonalds. And finally, and probably most importantly, they **enhanced** the food. Food is prepared daily, in-store from locally sourced produce.

People

The key to success in property is location, location and location. For Prêt à Manger, the key to success is recruitment, recruitment and recruitment. They **enhanced** their approach to recruitment and hired 'happy people to make sandwiches', frequently foreign university graduates in the UK to learn English. Unlike the slap 'Happy to Help' badge on employees approach, Prêt encourages employees to let their personalities shine through and measures customer service using mystery shoppers – good results result in employee bonuses.

To put into practice their mindset of 'Good jobs for good people', they **enhanced** staff buy-in. Long-serving store managers have equity in the company and employees have a say on who is hired. Prospective employees work in store for a trial day, and the team decide if they are a suitable fit or not.

They also **reduced** staff working hours and the number of repetitive tasks which frontline workers have to do, thus increasing employee satisfaction. Long-serving store managers work few nights or weekends – a rarity in the restaurant business.

Financial

Prêt **left unchanged** the fast-food model of paying quickly for food at a central till, but because they had enhanced the product they could **enhance** the price: their sandwiches are a little more expensive. Unlike their competitors, Prêt spends very little on marketing and instead invests in people and product.

This £150 million revenue business is now set to take on the fast-food industry in the US – whether it will succeed or not remains to be seen, but they've certainly been revolutionary in their home market.

Now start to ROLE through your own company. We find that it's the 'R' and 'O' parts of this exercise which people find most difficult, so don't be shy when it comes to **omitting** or **outsourcing** activities – too often, a company's progress is held back by trying to do too many things, which are not complementary. Strive to focus – to do a few things really well, rather than a multitude of things in a mediocre way. Set limits on what you will and won't do.

Here are questions to help you ROLE through your four functional areas:

 CUSTOMER

Can you enhance the areas your customers value, and reduce/omit those deemed irrelevant? Can sales, marketing and support be enhanced? Can you reduce customers not in your sweet spot?

 PRODUCT

What features of your product could be omitted? Which could be enhanced? What could be outsourced? Could your product be enhanced by combining it with other companies' products?

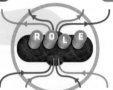

 PEOPLE

How can you enhance your staff's capability to beat the competition? What people activities can you reduce, omit, outsource, leave, or enhance? Does your company mindset need enhancing?

 FINANCE

How can revenue streams from customers be enhanced? How can your investments be reduced or enhanced? Through shared risk/shared reward? Are some of your current pricing strategies inefficient? Should discounts be omitted?

Beat the Competition Statement

The Beat the Competition Statement is always comparative and begins:
'Unlike the competition, we...'

The Beat the Competition statements of some company examples we've given in this chapter could go something like this:

University of Phoenix: 'Unlike other universities who educate young full-time students through a large, central campus, we further the education of working adults over 23 years of age, through small, convenient local campuses, and extensive eLearning.'

Zara: 'Unlike other fashion retailers who provide a maximum of four collections a year, manufactured in the Far East, we provide 'fast fashion' through mainly European-based manufacture, supported by young designers who create new fashions weekly, and a production system that gets cloth to high street in 10 days.'

Prêt à Manger: 'Unlike other fast-food companies which offer unhealthy food and don't focus on staff satisfaction, we prioritise healthy food and happy staff, without stinting on fast delivery times.'

Beat the Competition Case Study
Venus, Telecoms Software

A telecoms software client of ours, let's call them *Venus*, started losing deals against an Indian competitor, which was leveraging its low-cost location to offer cut-price solutions. Both companies were bidding to provide software solutions to large European telecoms operators. *Venus* could not match the Indian company on price and clients saw little difference in the product functionality being offered by the two companies. *Venus'* sales force was screaming at company management to reduce price.

Understand how your industry competes

We spoke to prospective customers, and industry experts, using the types of questions /methods suggested earlier in the chapter to try to understand how the industry competed and what it took to win in the sector. We found that the single biggest issue influencing the buying decision was not labour cost at all, but risk.

Many of the telecoms customers at some stage had purchased expensive software systems which they had never implemented, for a multitude of reasons. The conservative customers we spoke to were concerned about their own reputations should they be responsible for a failed project and wasted investment. A project delay by even a few months was very expensive for these telecom operators.

ROLE Reversal

Having identified the main customer concern as risk, we worked with *Venus* to address it. This meant changing the activities in ways that the Indian and other competitors would find it hard to match. We ROLE-d through the four functional areas:

Customers

Venus **reduced** prospective customers to telecoms operators in European countries where risk, rather than cost, was at the top of the agenda. It found its sweet spot.

Venus **enhanced** demonstration facilities which allowed customers to see evidence of the product working using their own data, thus reducing risk perception. *Venus* knew that they would be able to set up this demo with customer data in two days, but were aware that their competitors probably wouldn't be able to do so. They encouraged prospective customers to have a 'bake-off' (demanding all competitors set up demos). This successfully wrong-footed the Indian competitors.

Venus **enhanced** their marketing presence and positioned themselves as the safe option and as the only company which would guarantee that customers would be operational within six months.

Product

Venus's services charge-out rates were under real pressure, due to comparison with Indian charge-out rates. *Venus* was able to **reduce** its charge-out rates through **outsourcing** to an Eastern European services company that could provide better response times for support and additional service requests.

Venus **reduced** product features as their market was now more focussed

Venus traditional support for product breakdown was just during office hours. *Venus* **enhanced** this 24/7 support (at a higher fee) to reassure the risk conscious customers.

People

Venus hired in-country telecom software specialists to reassure clients of their expertise to address specific risk issues. They also introduced account managers **to enhance** their sales process, and reassure prospects that they would have a senior single point of contact responsible for the project, rather than be relying on a salesman who was off trying to win his next contract.

Finance

Venus moved its financial model to one of partially shared risk/shared reward, which was viewed as a big **enhancement by customers**.

Beat the Competition Statement

> *'Unlike other suppliers who have long project lead times we guarantee that our system will be operational within six months of contract signature. Our shared risk/shared reward commercial terms reflect this commitment to our joint success.'*

The good news is that this new approach wrong-footed the Indian and other competitors and put *Venus* on a new growth path.

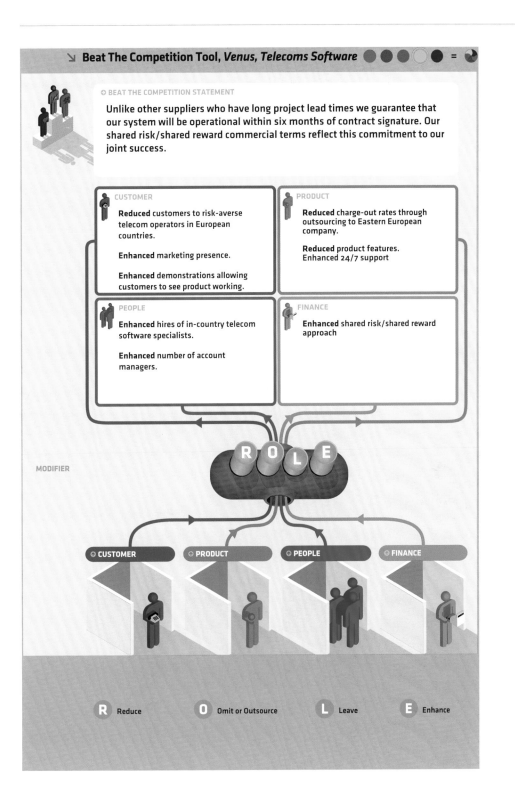

↘ **Beat The Competition Tool,** *Venus, Telecoms Software*

◉ BEAT THE COMPETITION STATEMENT

Unlike other suppliers who have long project lead times we guarantee that our system will be operational within six months of contract signature. Our shared risk/shared reward commercial terms reflect this commitment to our joint success.

CUSTOMER

Reduced customers to risk-averse telecom operators in European countries.

Enhanced marketing presence.

Enhanced demonstrations allowing customers to see product working.

PRODUCT

Reduced charge-out rates through outsourcing to Eastern European company.

Reduced product features.
Enhanced 24/7 support

PEOPLE

Enhanced hires of in-country telecom software specialists.

Enhanced number of account managers.

FINANCE

Enhanced shared risk/shared reward approach

R O L E

MODIFIER

◉ CUSTOMER   ◉ PRODUCT   ◉ PEOPLE   ◉ FINANCE

R Reduce   **O** Omit or Outsource   **L** Leave   **E** Enhance

Remember you can find ways to differentiate yourself and beat the competition at every step of anticipating and meeting customer needs. In the next chapter we look at how you get your product to market, and how to beat the competition by **cracking the channel code**.

↘ **Introduction**

↘ **Commit to a Shared Vision**

↘ **Select your Sweet Spot Customer**

↘ **Create Measurable Value**

↘ **Beat the Competition**

➔ **Crack the Channel Code**

↘ **Execute The Business Battlecard™**

'...the global winners over the next ten to twenty years are going to be the companies with the best distribution organizations that also provide superb customer support. Engineering excellence, manufacturing efficiency, and quality are rapidly becoming givens; everyone is going to need them to become a player.'

Donald V. Fites, former Chairman and CEO, Caterpillar

A client of ours, let's call them *Orion*, was building a software product that helped companies automate their sales, marketing and customer support functions. Their product offering was similar to Salesforce.com's original offering, and was highly useful because many mid-sized businesses find it hard to carry out such functions efficiently.

Our client debated a number of options about the best way to get their product to customers including: the traditional **direct sales** model, where the solution would be installed in the client's premises and the client would pay an upfront license fee and annual support fees; a **hosted solution**, allowing customers access the service over the internet and pay a small monthly fee; or giving the product away for free (in an **open source model**) and making money on services from each client.

Each option had its champions. The traditionalists argued for direct selling and wanted steady growth with hefty license fees for each sale. They wanted fast revenue growth and were prepared to invest heavily in recruiting top sales people to win sales. They were concentrating on attracting customers from banks and other financial institutions.

The hosted option proponents argued that the service was so easy to adopt that it didn't need a direct sales force; customers would have no difficulty accessing and buying through the internet. They wanted to invest heavily in a web presence and drive prospective customers to their website, where they could trial and later buy the product.

The revolutionaries pointed to Red Hat (one of the first companies to give their software away for free and make money on services) and wanted to become the open standard for this category of sales automation software. They felt the company could make money from selling follow-on services, once the product had an established customer base.

In the end, our client went the hosted solution route. Time will tell whether they made the right choice. What would have been a simple decision a decade ago is simple no longer. There are more options than ever in getting a product to market; this means exciting opportunities but also daunting choices.

Sales success for good products delivered through traditional channels used to be well-defined. Effectively, you built products, either sold them yourselves or went to a sales partner. The reseller made some margin, you made a profit, the customer got what they wanted, and everybody was happy. This has all changed.

Product is no longer king. Beating the competition with better products is a battle plan only for the brave.

Product is no longer king. Beating the competition with better products is a battle plan only for the brave. We can't all be Steve Jobs. Globalisation has driven the 'time to copy' down from years to weeks in some sectors and there is no going back. You may have the best product or service around but if you don't market, sell, distribute and support it properly, it will remain on the shelf. It's no longer what you sell but how you sell it. Today channels are the new drivers of revenue growth.

It's no longer what you sell but how you sell it. Today channels are the new drivers of revenue growth.

We are in a radical period for delivery and distribution of products and services. To survive and prosper, some companies have formed alliances and partnerships with their biggest enemies, others have broken off with their best friends. Seen one way, this has been a period of new channels, and new and sometimes surprising relationships. Seen another way it has been a period when all roads lead to the internet. Seen all ways, the question 'How do I get my product to customers?' has become more complex.

Channels are not a tactical add on, they are a fundamental part of your **Business Battlecard**, and they will change as the market evolves and as your company matures.

What Is A Channel?

First, what is a channel? A channel is any route that helps you get your products to customers. Whilst products and value propositions are about **what** you sell, channels are all about **how** you sell.

A channel is any route that helps you get your products to customers.

Developing channels is about building complete sales activity across your chosen markets. The nature of your offering, its price point, and the broadness of its potential market reach will drive you towards particular channel options. For clarity we classify all channels into just three types:

- Direct (for example your own sales team);
- Indirect (for example partners, resellers);
- The Internet (for example websites, search engines, social networking tools, new delivery mechanisms).

Like all growing companies, you are faced with challenges: Which channel should you use? Should you hire a direct sales team? Should you focus your direct sales team only on big ticket deals and use lower cost channels to win smaller deals? Should you seek agents in local territories? How will bringing in outside sales agents conflict with your own sales resources? How will you find channel partners who want to work with you? What role should the internet play?

Answering one of these questions doesn't mean you can avoid the rest. Channel selection is not about choosing one channel and cutting out others. Successful companies juggle channels and don't rely exclusively on one route to market. For instance *Orion* invested heavily in their web presence, but they still needed both a direct sales force and channel partners to drive growth.

Many companies leave the channel discussion until after they've achieved a certain size, but channels now are a cornerstone of strategy and should be considered from the outset. One of the reasons why companies get trapped under a glass ceiling is that they haven't cracked the channel code. If you have a great product but the wrong channel code you're not going to grow.

Crack the Channel Code

Like the Da Vinci Code, the channel code is not easy to crack. Channels are full of conflict, twists and turns, great expectations, broken promises and just when you think you've got one cracked, the market changes and you're trying to crack a new sequence to the code.

Even the giants of industry make mistakes. Former poster child of the direct over the internet model, Dell Computers, had to go sucking back to resellers and distributors to complement its direct coverage and help it get its products to more customers.

Few companies have products or services with broad appeal to all sales or delivery channels. Concentrating on those channels which best get your products to customers is critical to efficiency. Only where the wheels of your engine mesh smoothly with the cogs of the channels' power plant should you expend energy. This is where channel choices support your shared vision, direct you to sweet spot customers, enhance the value you offer and help you beat the competition.

Only where the wheels of your engine mesh smoothly with the cogs of the channels' power plant should you expend energy.

Your channel code is dependent, first, on where your product is on the market lifecycle. Is it at the introductory, growth, or maturity stage? Figure this out because each stage needs a different code. Secondly, your channel code is dependent on how the customer chooses to buy your product. From lead generation right through to post-sales support, each selling stage requires particular channel choices. And finally, factor in your ambition – are you looking to sell locally, or globally? If, like many companies, you're selling in separate territories, you may need a different channel code for each territory

Cracking the channel code takes time and careful planning. The good news is that once you've got it right, the next time will be easier, because you'll understand what role market lifecycle, the selling process and ambition play in cracking the code.

Channels are too complex for a simple score card of pluses and minuses on the different options. Overly simplistic and tactical models have created a shaky foundation upon which most channels programmes are based. Channel choices affect the way you build products, design services and hire people. Forward-looking companies grow fast using hybrid models which help them move more successfully though their sales cycles. This chapter helps you crack the channel code by showing you how to understand the market, the customer, the territory and the sales cycle. It covers:

* The **three channel types** and how to manage them;
* Understanding **the market lifecycle** and getting your product channel-ready;
* Understanding the **sales cycle** by getting inside the buyer's mind;
* Crafting your **channel code statement**.

Use the Channel Code Tool to help you select the best mix of channels to drive growth.

↘ **Channel Code Tool**   ● ● ● ● ◉ = ◗

	DIRECT	INDIRECT	INTERNET
⊙ SALES OBJECTIVE			
Lead Generation			
Qualification			
Proposal			
Acquisition/Close			
Support			

Channel Code Statement

The Three Channel Types

The three main channel types are: direct, indirect, and internet. Most of your selling will be a mix of these three.

Direct Channel

Your direct channel is your own sales team. It's the most knowledgeable and committed resource you have. A direct sales force is the most expensive way to sell but you will often have little option when introducing new products. Focus your direct sales force on winning major deals, leaving smaller deals to be managed by other channels.

As covered in chapter 3, your sales people must be able to create rather than just *communicate* value for customers.

Indirect Channels

An indirect channel is any intermediary that helps you sell and make your products available to customers. It includes distributors, resellers, consultants, system integrators, influencers and lots of industry-specific partner types.

Many companies lament their lack of control over channel partners and resent sharing revenue, but indirect channels help you get products to customers that you would never get to on your own. It's better to have a small slice of a big cake than a little cake all to yourself. Channel partners can often combine your product with their own or with another company's to give the customer the solution they truly want. And established channel partners can bring credibility and introductions to large customers.

Building a good indirect sales channel is hard work but if you invest time and effort it can be the route to growth. Make no mistake, indirect channels are important – in the technology sector for example, indirect channels account for over 70% of all sales.

Managing channel partners

When you sign up your first big channel partner the future looks rosy. Promises have been made, growth looks inevitable and investors are happy. But how can you ensure that this partnership delivers on your expectations?

First, some home truths: most channel partners will not be as excited as you are about your product or as patient about seeking revenue opportunities. Their sales people will fast lose interest if deals are not closed quickly.

Most channel partners are service-led and are looking for ways to generate additional revenue from new products. Some may want to add your product to their portfolio to deliver a complete solution to their customers, to win more deals. Others may be looking for a recurring revenue stream from your product.

Try to understand how channel partners make money. Understand the way they motivate their sales people. Figure out the level of revenue that your product needs to generate for them. Seek channel partners who have an implicit need for your product. Try to understand whether selling your product gives them a clear weapon to beat their competitors with.

Before you approach potential channel partners, remember that they will be sizing you up as well. Use aspects of your Business Battlecard to demonstrate your strengths and help get them engaged.

Seek channel partners who have an implicit need for your product. Try to understand whether selling your product gives them a clear weapon to beat their competitors with.

Customer Service: *Lexus*

Lexus is the luxury car division of Toyota. Now the highest seller of luxury cars in the US, Lexus was sneered at by media pundits in 1989, as it sought to compete in the high-end market, dominated by Mercedes and BMW. Lexus imitated the best of German engineering (ok slightly better!) but that doesn't explain its success. Its exclusive and highly profitably dealerships were at the core of its successful growth strategy. Lexus chose dealers with a real customer service mindset, who ensured that the Lexus ownership experience was unrivalled. Understanding the value of having enthusiastic and trusted channel partners helped Lexus steal a march on their product-driven competitors. Lexus accounts for less than 3% of all passenger cars produced by Toyota, but 30% of profits!

Internet

The internet has made cracking the channel code simultaneously easier and more challenging. It extends your reach at a fraction of the cost of other channels, and potentially gives start-up companies access to customers that traditional channels would never reach. But with an increasingly congested web, getting your message through requires precision, cunning, and speed of execution. Your message has to be razor-sharp and get to exactly the right people.

Lead generation options like Google Search and blogs, and information sharing and business networking tools like LinkedIn can strengthen and extend your network of trusted contacts, if adroitly handled. It's not a question of whether you are using tools like this – it's how well you are using them.

Motivating employees: *Globoforce*

Globoforce helps the world's largest companies motivate their employees. It makes it easy for managers in large companies (10,000+ employees) to say 'thank you' to employees with a simple on demand, web-based gift service. It enables them deliver a culturally relevant personalised thank you gift, on a timely basis, anywhere in the world. Globoforce had a shared vision about the reward and recognition market and has created a new delivery model, with relationships with over 2000 merchants worldwide.

While selling direct is Globoforce's main sales channel, the internet is crucial every step of the way. From blog, to cartoon examples of employee recognition gone wrong, to webinars which educate buyers, to whitepapers which help buyers make the business case for their solution – all play a part in generating new leads, educating and vetting buyers and helping them sell the proposition internally.

Cracking the channel code has enabled Globoforce become the world's leading provider of recognition programmes for Global 2000 companies.

How good is your website? This may seem a blindingly obvious question, but a company we worked with had a brilliant product and brilliant people on board but failed to secure a major contract. When we asked the customer why not, they said that our client's website had seemed so amateur that the CEO didn't want to have anything to do with them. Don't get caught out – whatever channel you're concentrating on, your web presence needs to be up to scratch. Your reputation lives on the internet.

Your reputation lives on the internet.

Understand the Market Lifecycle

The next point to consider is the stage of development of the market. As outlined in Chapter 2, there are three main growth phases of market development: **introduction**, **growth** and **maturity**. Customers can be segmented by their position in the lifecycle as early adopters, pragmatists or conservatives/sceptics.

Introductory phase – pitching to early adopters

With a new product, the customer will be wary and will require lots of assurances. A direct evangelical sales force is often the best option, supported by internet selling, and possibly also loosely by partners to help provide credibility. Be prepared for a long buying cycle.

At this stage, you're aiming at early adopters, and the more innovative the product, the more willing to take a plunge the customer needs to be. Don't waste time selling to cautious companies who only ever get involved at the mature stage. Price is not a determining factor – the early adopters go for your product because they like being first off the block. Early adopters aren't penny-pinchers.

Early adopters aren't penny-pinchers.

Growth – convincing the pragmatists

During the growth phase savvy customers become more knowledgeable and put downward pressure on prices. Being pragmatists, they're not about to adopt any product unless they're convinced of its usefulness. At this stage, indirect channel partners are often the best option. They provide you with the additional market coverage you'll need. A channel partner who understands the customer and knows how to present your product could be the difference between winning and losing. It's worth sharing revenue.

Maturity – going online with conservatives

During maturity, growth slows and margins deteriorate. Conservative customers have accepted the need for the product. Product standards emerge and products become commoditised. The opportunity for sales (direct or indirect) to create value for the customer is limited. While large customers may still place some value on an account management-type relationship, many simply want a transactional-type purchase, with minimal contact. Competitors with low cost channels and high coverage will be the strongest.

Examples of maturity include travel and accommodation, which were once the preserve of travel agents, but have now moved mainly to low-cost internet channels. Similarly, markets for many food stuffs have moved to the commodity hell of quoting on internet auctions.

If you are in maturing markets, learn the lesson of the frog, which was put in very gradually heating water. It did not notice the water heating up, until it gradually died.

If you are in maturing markets, learn the lesson of the frog, which was put in very gradually heating water. It did not notice the water heating up, until it gradually died. Unlike the frog, anticipate the future and either differentiate yourself fast from the competition or start moving to lower cost channels.

Channel hopping and product tweaking

As the market lifecycle changes, you will find yourself channel hopping and may need to change your channels. Be aware that as you channel hop, you will have to tweak your product to meet the requirements of your new channel.

Be aware that as you channel hop, you will have to tweak your product to meet the requirements of your new channel.

When considering whether your product is channel ready, think about it from the customer and channel partner perspective. If you have a complex product and you are moving towards a lower-cost channel, consider simplifying it. If the customer is bewildered with lots of features, they will require a lot handholding. So, reduce the number of features, make your product easy to understand and use. Think about shrink-wrapping. Simplify your pricing.

Your channel approach affects each of the key areas of your company. Sales and marketing need to ensure that their message is on-target and in tune with channel partners; Engineering will need to ensure that the product can be delivered efficiently through the chosen channel; and Finance will almost certainly need to tweak pricing as the market changes.

A software client of ours, Similarity Systems, had a terrific product idea, which solved data quality problems in large corporations. Prior to building the product, the CEO tested the concept with potential channel partners. He took on board their feedback and revised the product concept to help these potential partners make a lot of money. When Similarity Systems launched their product the channel partners were able to bring on board a set of customers that an early stage company could only dream of.

The following illustrative table matches channel and product to market lifecycle:

Market lifecycle	Best channel option	Product
Introduction	Direct sales force (in-house or field). Internet.	Raw, exciting product needing lots of hand-holding. Price can be high.
Growth	Combination of direct to key customers & specialist channel partners to rest of market. Internet.	Part shrink-wrapped, part-customised; factor in some cost-savings.
Maturity	Direct account management with large customers; technical specialist partners with customers who still require technical expertise; and broad-based (web- and phone-driven) limited technical support for remainder.	Shrink-wrapped and cheap.

What stage is your product at in the market lifecycle?

What criteria should you use to determine suitable channel partners? What resources would you expect them to provide?

What actions do you need to take to adapt your product to your channel? Should your product be simplified?

Understand the Sales Cycle

Each of the four steps so far in our **Business Battlecard** has the customer at its core. It is no different for channel – the customer is king when it comes to choosing channel. Ask yourself: 'Which mix of channels creates the most value for our customers?'.

The customer is king when it comes to choosing channel.

Try to understand how the customer buys. What do the buyers need at each step along the way to buying from you? Remember this is separate from what you think they might need.

Speaking to a senior corporate buyer recently, we were reminded of the extent of the 'perspective gap' between the buying and the selling communities. This senior buyer invested time in educating his team on how to handle vendors. He counselled them not to build too close a relationship with the sales person; to understand vendors' positioning tactics; to apply competitive pressure to keep suppliers focused, and to manage the communication process to make sure that they, as buyers, were the ones controlling the procedure. This included keeping senior executives away from vendors until a chosen point in the cycle.

What struck us about this process was the level of built-in planning. Professional buyers know every step they want to take in the buying cycle. They have a detailed project plan, complete with hurdles and obstacles. Unless you, the vendor, can visualize the journey they want to take, and have your own map to get there, you won't be with them when they reach their destination.

Let's face it - if growing companies are an opportunity for corporate buyers, they're also a risk. No-one ever got fired for buying from IBM, but if a procurement manager purchases from a start-up and it goes bust, then his job could well be on the line.

Corporate buyers are concerned with managing the significant risks associated with purchasing. Choose the channel options which will reassure the buyer.

Corporate buyers are concerned not only with managing the buying process, but also with managing the significant risks associated with purchasing. A part of your job is to choose the channel options which will reassure the buyer.

To crack the channel code, think about your sales cycle as carefully as the corporate buyer does, and with the same level of in-built planning. Look at the channel options your competitors are using and evaluate what's working for them and what's not.

The combination to crack the channel code has multiple sets of variables. You have already considered where your product is in the market lifecycle. You've looked at tweaking it to make it more channel ready. You've considered the buyer's perspective. Now you just have to match the stage of the sales cycle (lead-generation, qualification, proposal, acquisition /close and post-sale support) to type of channel. Each stage involves choices. Make the right choices and you've cracked the channel code, leading to strong growth.

You will find yourself channel hopping as you move through the sales cycle. You might begin generating leads through the internet, before moving to aggressive direct selling at the next stage, and later involving channel partners to reduce perceived risk. Cracking the channel code is dependent on understanding exactly which channel is needed for each stage of the sales cycle.

This topic is dealt with in more detail in our book *Select Selling* (co-authored with Donal Daly). For clarity's sake, we identify five stages to the sales cycle:

1. Lead-generation: The goal is to make initial contact with prospective customers. There are a lot of ways to do this, but the internet is an ideal low cost channel, if properly handled. Think about Google advertising to draw prospective customers to your website, or more traditional ways like seminars, telesales or 'dialling for dollars'. The method needs to be appropriate to the buyers' way of searching.

2. Qualification: The goal is to assess the likelihood of a sale. After checking that a prospect is in your sweet spot, create ways of testing whether they intend buying from you. Clearly a professional sales person, armed with the right set of questions is one option but this is often expensive, particularly for face-to-face meetings. A well-informed channel partner who has done business with this customer may also be an option. Qualification is continuous throughout the sales process and each channel option should play its part.

3. Proposal: Your goal is to use all the information you've gleaned to position your offering as the winning one.

Before creating a proposal, you'll want to understand more about the customers requirements, possibly meeting the prospective customer directly, using a channel partner, or devising a way to capture the requirements over the internet – each being an option depending on the stage your company is at, how the buyer buys and how much you are prepared to invest.

You may consider using channels to drive home how much better you are than the competition – like Lexus with its superb dealers and their special customer service mindset.

As part of the proposal stage, the buyer will want evidence that you can deliver on your promises and that your product is all it's cracked up to be. Credible channel partners, product demonstrations, and a strong website are all ways of reassuring the customer.

Credible channel partners, product demonstrations, and a strong website are all ways of reassuring the customer.

4. Acquisition/Close: At the acquisition and closing stage, particularly for big deals, you have to be there in person. Risk will be uppermost in the buyer's mind – they often feel a bit trapped. Concessions will be asked for, new objections may be raised and price reductions sought. Failure to get the deal across the line will be costly and disappointing. A channel partner whom the buyer trusts could be a good option.

5. Post-sales support: Your goal is to ensure a happy customer and prove to them that they made the right decision. You may have a high, direct relationship with the customer during early implementation. Partners may take this over and as customers become self-sufficient web support may be all that's required.

> **How do buyers go about searching for products like yours? Where do they look? Who do they ask?**
>
> **What channel (direct, indirect channel or internet) is best to qualify whether their interest is real?**
>
> **What is the best way to gather enough information and position yourself to win with the client (direct, indirect or internet)?**
>
> **What is the best channel to use to close and support prospects, post sale?**

Channel Code Statement

Now start encapsulating your channel strategy into a channel code statement. It should build on the following phrases:

- 'We have chosen these channels to market for our product because...'
- 'The benefit to our channel partners is...'
- 'Our channels provide the following additional value to our customers...'

Lexus
'We adopt a premium brand approach, supported by customer-intimate dealers to generate good profits for both ourselves and our partners which we continually reinvest in the brand.'

Globoforce
'We have a direct sales channel, where professional sales people sell to senior decision makers, in our sweet spot of the top 2000 Global companies worldwide. Our website supports our direct sales efforts by generating leads and educating buyers regarding our solution.'

Channel Code Case Study
Steeltrace, requirements management software application

A client of ours, SteelTrace, based in Dublin, built a product that helped software project managers with complex projects. The application helped prevent project failures, often costing millions of dollars so its potential was huge. SteelTrace's application appealed to sectors like technology, telecoms, and government, and across most geographic markets.

However at the early stage of the company, the product was priced at $15,000 and could not be sold profitably through a direct field sales force.

Here's how SteelTrace cracked the channel code:

1. **Lead generation**: The key buyers for this type of product were technical project managers. Getting the requirements wrong could mean disaster for their projects. They would typically search the internet for solutions. So SteelTrace used paid Google advertisement words, using the terms 'requirements management' to drive prospects to their website.

2. **Qualification**: On the SteelTrace website, prospects were given a 'try before you buy' option, after they had been vetted via specially crafted telephone sales qualification. They were allowed to download the product from SteelTrace's website and put their own data into the product so they could see the benefits for themselves. The 'try before you buy' option lasted 10 days before the next phase of the sales cycle.

3. Proposal: After further exploratory discussions with prospective customers, a proposal was crafted by experienced telesales professionals who summarising the client need, supporting it with key SteelTrace differentiators, demonstrating its unique value. To reassure prospects for larger deals, SteelTrace used established local partners.

4. Acquisition/Close: For modest deal sizes, deals were completed over the phone. The hard work had been done through the 'try before you buy' approach and the rigorous qualification process adopted. For larger deals, local partners were retained.

5. Post sales support: Provided over the web and through telephone support. This support proved to be more than adequate for technical users, who were using a stable, mature product.

SteelTrace cracked the channel code with a low-touch self-serve option and a short buying cycle.

SteelTrace's channel code statement

'Our key buyers are project managers who look to the web for solutions. We use Google ad words to drive prospects to our site, where they can see our product demo'd, followed by a "try before you buy" approach, after they have been vetted. We use professional telesales people armed with a disciplined sales process to win deals.'

When SteelTrace sought bigger sized deals as the company developed, it had to create a new channel mix to convince large corporate purchasers to spend hundreds of thousands of dollars for multiple copies of their products. It pursued an indirect channel partner model involving resellers and larger companies who packaged SteelTrace's product with theirs.

Steeltrace became a market leader in its segment and was recently acquired by Detroit based Compuware.

Channel Code Tool, *Steeltrace, requirements management software*

SALES OBJECTIVE	DIRECT	INDIRECT	INTERNET
Lead Generation			Google ad words, supported by website
Qualification	Professional sales qualification over phone		Demonstration/ 'try before you buy'
Proposal	Sales professional summarising discussions using standard proposal template.	Local partners for larger deals	
Acquisition/Close	Close deal and secure purchase order over the phone for modest deals	Local partners for larger deals	Licence key for 'try before you buy' expires – encouraging buying decision
Support	Telephone support		Provided over internet

Channel Code Statement

"Our key buyers are project managers who look to the web for solutions. We use Google ad words to drive prospects to our site, where they can see our product demo'd, followed by a 'try before you buy' approach, after they have been vetted. We use professional telesales people armed with a disciplined sales process to win deals."

↘ **Introduction**

↘ **Commit to a Shared Vision**

↘ **Select your Sweet Spot Customer**

↘ **Create Measurable Value**

↘ **Beat the Competition**

↘ **Crack the Channel Code**

● **Execute The Business Battlecard™**

'If I can't picture it. I can't understand it'

Albert Einstein.

A number of years ago, one of our client companies, let's call them *Pegasus* – a management consulting company with a broad range of clients, from very large to small – left our workshop with five completed tools on Shared Vision, Sweet Spot, Measurable Value, Beating the Competition and Channels. The whole team had worked together productively and we were confident that they now had the means to put a winning strategy in place and to turn round their fortunes. Recently we revisited them. They had grown significantly and there was more clarity about the direction they were taking. Their management team had made tough decisions, for instance phasing out the smaller clients to concentrate solely on larger ones. They were pleased with progress; however to realise the shared vision they had set themselves two years ago, they needed to have another look at their strategy.

When we talked to the management team, considered new customers they'd won and looked at business performance, we found that through focussing on the tools *Pegasus* had learnt a lot and were stronger as a company. However while work on each separate tool was strong, where they were lacking was in integration, linkage and alignment. For instance they had improved sweet spot, but their internet presence was ineffective in winning and servicing their newly targeted sweet spot clients. They were much clearer on the measurable value they delivered, but weren't feeding that value into beating the competition.

The five tools are mutually interdependent and reinforce each other – we convey this on the Battlecard through the central image of the swirling pie-chart, which we term the **virtuous circle**. If you removed one segment from this virtuous circle, it wouldn't roll. The way to put velocity into the circle is to get the five tools working in synch. Any adjustment you make to one tool has repercussions on all the others. If sweet spot changes it has knock-on effects on shared vision, measurable value, beat the competition and channels.

The other problem *Pegasus* was encountering was in executing their strategy. They hadn't applied sufficient discipline to the process. Some issues weren't getting the attention they needed and crucially, there was no structured and formal review process.

Until your tools are integrated, your strategy remains in pieces, like bits of jigsaw before they're fitted together; and until your strategy is executed, it's just nice words and images on a page.

Until your tools are aligned, your strategy remains in pieces, like bits of jigsaw before they're fitted together; and until your strategy is executed, it's just nice words and images on a page. Based on our experience with *Pegasus*, we've come up with an approach to help you align and execute your strategy:

- Integrate your five tools on the **Business Battlecard** and get them working together in a **virtuous circle**;
- Set **basecamps** to help execute the Battlecard.

The Business Battlecard

⬊ Business Battlecard™
Winning moves for growing companies

⬤⬤⬤⬤⬤ =

1 SHARED VISION
What do you want to be famous for?

2 SWEET SPOT
Who are your selected customers?

5 CHANNELS
How will you get your product to market?

3 MEASURABLE VALUE
Where is your measurable value?

4 BEAT THE COMPETITION
Why should customers choose you rather than your competitors?

The Business Battlecard is a trademark of Select Strategies.

The Business Battlecard pulls together the work that you have undertaken from the other chapters onto one PowerPoint. It takes the essence of each of the five tools – the Shared Vision Statement, the Sweet Spot Statement, the Measurable Value Statement, the Beat the Competition Statement and the Channel Code Statement – and brings them together, emphasizing through the image of the **virtuous circle**, their interdependence and the extent to which they mutually reinforce each other.

The Business Battlecard is the clearest and simplest depiction of the strategy you've created with your team, and is the basis of communicating that strategy. It shows what you stand for, and what you don't.

Create a virtuous rather than a vicious circle

You've heard of a 'vicious circle' – it's when you do one thing badly, which leads to doing the next thing worse. In our experience non-aligned and incommunicable strategies are the main reason for vicious circles developing in growing companies. In contrast, we think of the Business Battlecard as favouring a **virtuous circle**. When your strategy is working, and all five tools are mutually reinforcing each other, then all the wheels and cogs of your company are turning in tandem: you're in a virtuous circle and you're moving forward.

When your strategy is working, and all five tools are mutually reinforcing each other, then all the wheels and cogs of your company are turning in tandem: you're in a virtuous circle and you're moving forward.

The virtuous circle in action: *McKinsey & Company*

Global strategy consulting firm, McKinsey & Company is a good example of the virtuous circle in action: from their sweet spot focus on Fortune 100 companies and governments, to their prestige image much sought after by the bright MBAs they recruit and train in their codified consulting toolkits, to their ability to suck information from their clients and perform rigorous analysis, to their high level sales process, using McKinsey alumni to help them win the business. McKinsey's €3 billion in revenue and 10,000 employees is testimony to a virtuous circle in action.

McKinsey – although obviously a much larger company – was a good role model for *Pegasus*. The dynamic way in which each area of McKinsey's business feeds into and reinforces all the other areas helps create velocity and self-perpetuating momentum. Companies that execute the Battlecard well are on their way to achieving this.

Every aspect of leadership, sales, marketing and delivery must support and drive home the chosen strategy. You'll recall from examples given in the previous chapters, how successful companies like Prêt à Manger and Zara devised their strategies, so that all areas of business were mutually reinforcing. There was consistency between product, customer, people and finance. Such consistency is the cornerstone of successful companies, and this is what the Business Battlecard helps you to achieve.

The Battlecard brings your internal strategy together onto one PowerPoint, making it easy to see how the different elements relate to each other, and how all actions have a knock-on effect.

For instance, if new opportunities appear, you can test them via the Battlecard. When considering a new set of customers, you can test whether the existing value you offer still applies, whether this new segment values your offerings in the same way as your existing customers, whether you now have new competitors, and whether you need to consider new channel partners.

Through continuous use of the Battlecard, it becomes second nature to test the effect of any new action on your shared vision, your sweet spot customers, your measurable value, your channels and your ability to beat the competition. Theoretically you know that by changing one way of doing things, you change another, but when actions are compartmentalised, this truism is easy to forget.

Too often, we see companies drift towards new customer segments. Suddenly they're competing on new rules against new competitors that they have not prepared themselves to fight against. Before they know it, their strategy has become misaligned and incommunicable. The Business Battlecard prevents strategy drift.

Get buy-in from your team

You've a better chance of buy-in when the whole team has invested in the strategy and so feels ownership of, and emotional commitment towards, it. The strategy hasn't been imposed on them; they've built it themselves. The Business Battlecard makes strategy creation a continuous process owned, not just by top management, but by the whole company.

The key members of your team have worked through the five tools to create the Battlecard. This process has given them new insights into their customers, their colleagues' opinions

The Business Battlecard makes strategy creation a continuous process owned, not just by top management, but by the whole company.

and company objectives. It has encouraged them to break out of their separate silos to consider their colleagues' perspectives and the needs of the company as a whole. After completing the Battlecard, sales feel ownership not just of sweet spot, but of mindset, and engineering not just of product, but of distinctive competencies and finding ways to beat the competition.

Balance opportunism with discipline

In our experience, many companies fail at the execution stage because the strategy was too hard to understand by those who had to execute it. The advantage of the Battlecard approach is that the discipline involved, and the final depiction on one PowerPoint, make the strategy clear to all who will be involved in its execution. By working through the Battlecard, you create a common language, a common set of tools and a common framework that allows people to think through the implications of the day-to-day challenges that they face. It puts a set of strategic thinking tools within the mindset of the whole team, and helps make strategic thinking everybody's day job.

For growing companies, there's a dynamic in the external market that's ever-changing, and the temptation is to seize every opportunity. The Battlecard imposes discipline and forces hard questions. After weighing things up, via the Battlecard, your team might well conclude that there is a new set of customers, but that as a company you've no competitive advantage so shouldn't go there.

The Battlecard doesn't stilt creativity or opportunism, but it puts a discipline on the process. Don't leap without looking. The beauty of the Battlecard is its simplicity – it's a quick tool you can react with to new circumstances.

Set Basecamps

Imagine a group of mountaineers scaling Everest. Their aim is to reach the summit but they know they'll never do it in one go, so they devise a series of basecamps, which serve as stopping points to allow for altitude acclimatisation, to recalculate the risks, to check whether they're on the right path, and to mentally prepare for the next phase of the ascent.

Robert Burgelman, professor at Stanford Business School, uses the basecamp metaphor for growing companies. Building your company is a lot like climbing Everest. The summit is far away. Setting yourself and your team basecamps along the path provides clear short-term goals to strive towards.

Building your company is a lot like climbing Everest. The summit is far away. Setting yourself and your team basecamps along the path provides clear short-term goals to strive towards.

After completing the five tools and integrating them on the Battlecard, your team will go back to their day jobs. They'll inevitably be swallowed up by the operational detail of day-to-day firefighting. Consumed by activity, it can be hard to focus on strategy.

Basecamp objectives are the critical things that need to be accomplished to prove to the team that the strategic direction is the right one. Reaching basecamp tells the team that they have moved forward and are on the right path. If they don't reach basecamp, something's wrong.

Betting on the future is risky. Big companies can weather strategy failure, and regularly do, but for a growing company it can be fatal.

Growth companies can't just extrapolate the results from past experience and they've limited resources to test things out. They have to make do with assumptions, and business lore tells us that assumptions made about the future are often wrong.

At basecamp you test whether the assumptions on which you've based your strategy still hold. Basecamps serve as a checkpoint to test and refine strategy and evaluate progress in executing the Battlecard.

At basecamp you test whether the assumptions on which you've based your strategy still hold. Basecamps serve as a checkpoint to test and refine strategy and evaluate progress in executing the Battlecard.

Basecamps ensure strategy follow through. It can be hard to maintain focus, and basecamps introduce discipline and keep focus on the critical items that must be achieved.

Basecamps prove especially useful when there are conflicting views about the strategy laid out on a Battlecard. Nay-sayers are against ambitious plans, but because the objectives are concrete, and the time-frame is short, and the amount of investment is modest, even the sceptics will agree to setting a basecamp three months away. Basecamps allow for small bets or experiments that provide you with the information to devise a more informed strategy.

Setting basecamp objectives

When selecting your basecamp objectives, ask these questions: given the strategy laid out in the Business Battlecard, what would success look like in three months? What are the critical things we need to have accomplished? What are the proofs we need to show that our strategy is working, and to give us the confidence that we should put more resources behind the strategy?

Basecamps are set one at a time, and the team that created the Battlecard sets the basecamps, with the CEO driving. Your first basecamp will emerge from the Battlecard, and will be tailored to your particular company needs. It isn't a question of one basecamp fitting all. There are many ways to climb Everest. The basecamps should:

- Be challenging enough to stretch the team but be achievable within existing resources;
- Set the foundation for the creation of the next higher level basecamp;
- Be linked to ensure execution of the Battlecard;
- And the first basecamp should be no more than three to six months ahead.

As we've emphasized throughout this book, growing your company depends not just on improving your product but on improving all areas of your business. So when setting basecamps it's helpful to look at the four key company areas and devise objectives for each of them.

Your basecamp objectives could be laid out in the following way:

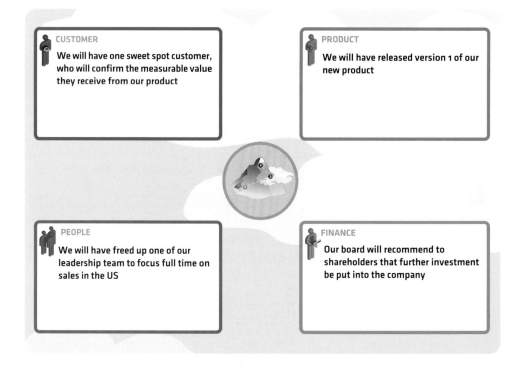

CUSTOMER
We will have one sweet spot customer, who will confirm the measurable value they receive from our product

PRODUCT
We will have released version 1 of our new product

PEOPLE
We will have freed up one of our leadership team to focus full time on sales in the US

FINANCE
Our board will recommend to shareholders that further investment be put into the company

After you've set the basecamps, ask your team to prepare action plans to take you there. Each key area will devise separate action plans, with their own specific targets and measurement systems, such as new customer wins, new product enhancements, and critical staff hires. After devising action plans, the whole team convenes to review the plans and ensure alignment towards the first basecamp.

Setting basecamps: *Adara*

A number of years ago, we were asked by a venture capital firm to do some work with an engineering company we'll called *Adara*. *Adara* was an engineering driven firm with a 'build it and they will come' mindset. Whilst their product had promise, the leadership had blinkers on. They had ambitious sales forecasts but refused to engage with potential customers until the product was 'right'. Meanwhile cash was running out and the venture capitalist's patience was running thin.

After some convincing, we helped the team craft a basecamp. To test their Business Battlecard, we decided what proofs of strategy were needed about *Adara* and the industry in which it competed. We sought to uncover the critical customer, product, people, and financial risks. The basecamp was set three months

CUSTOMER
...we will have secured two lead customers to work with our engineering team to deliver a product prototype.

PRODUCT
...our engineering team will have committed to delivering a product that's better than competitive offerings in the opinion of key customers.

PEOPLE
...one of our leadership team will be spending 100 percent of their time engaging directly with customers.

FINANCE
...we will meet our committed quarterly sales figures

away, at Christmas:
By *Adara's* first basecamp, they had achieved the first proofs of product and customer but whilst sales had improved, due to focus on customers, targets had been missed by a small margin. Their original Business Battlecard was revised and the go-ahead given for the project.

Adara got focussed, met its second basecamp targets (after some management changes) and is on the road to growth.

Basecamp review

Basecamps are a time for your team to gather together, review progress so far, assess whether the strategy is working, and to what extent it needs to be adjusted. They are a good time to look back and reflect on what has been learnt in the journey of moving your strategy forward.

Achieving the basecamp gives you proof that your strategy is working and that you have the right team for now. Once you have that proof, it justifies more resources being applied.

If you're off-target, ask yourself if this is because your strategy is inherently flawed, or because of unforeseen external market conditions, or because you set an unrealistic basecamp, or because you didn't have the right people in the right jobs? Examine your action plans and your Business Battlecard. Where did the problem occur? Delve deep. The most obvious explanation isn't always the right one. The good news is that whatever the reason, you are catching it early on and can take corrective action. By testing and learning, you are strengthening your strategy.

The basecamp review helps ensure that a bad strategy fails fast and a good one gets the resources it deserves.

The basecamp review helps ensure that a bad strategy fails fast and a good one gets the resources it deserves.

In our experience, the most likely outcome at basecamp is that you will have met some objectives, but not all of them. Generally your strategy won't need to be scrapped but will need adjusting. Most strategies need to be revised when they are put into action; measures and behaviours will need tweaking – because market conditions are changing all the time. At basecamp, ask your team the following questions:

* Is this still the correct strategy? What changes are required?
* What have we learnt? Are our assumptions still valid?
* How capable are we of executing this strategy?
* In getting to this basecamp, did we use up more resources than budgeted for?
* Have we the right structure, processes, compensation systems and measures in place to help execute the key tasks?
* Are we being too ambitious? Not ambitious enough?
* Is our current mindset suitable for execution of this plan? What behaviours need to change?
* Is each key person capable and motivated to execute this strategy?
* What new skills do we need?
* What are our competitors planning to do?

Be prepared to make tough decisions. You may find that existing skills are not quite right for what you are setting out to achieve. At this stage, it can be useful to get feedback from customers, members of the board, or industry experts.

To keep the Battlecard execution clearly on the agenda, a CEO of one of our clients regularly asks his executives: What have you done since the last basecamp? What will you do between now and next basecamp? What's getting in the way of you delivering on your promises? He will typically do this at the start of key meetings to keep the peer pressure on his team and make sure that there is focus and alignment.

The Business Battlecard
Salesforce.com

We've given the example of Salesforce.com a few times in this book. Here's how their Battlecard might look. We are providing it here for illustrative purposes only and it is not based on current detailed knowledge of Salesforce.com's strategy:

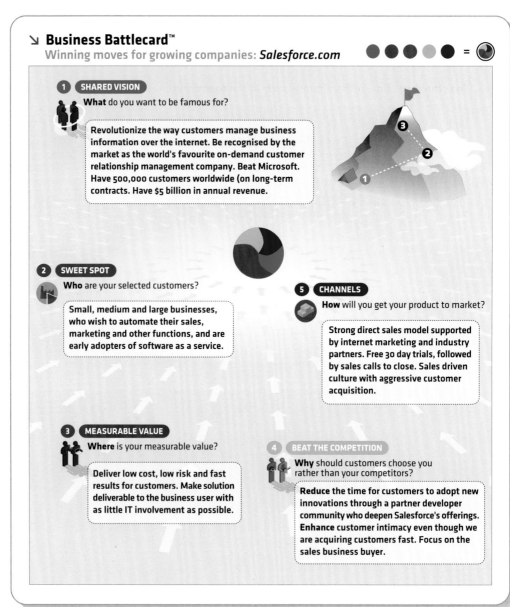

↘ **Business Battlecard**™
Winning moves for growing companies: *Salesforce.com*   ● ● ● ● ● = ◔

1 SHARED VISION

What do you want to be famous for?

Revolutionize the way customers manage business information over the internet. Be recognised by the market as the world's favourite on-demand customer relationship management company. Beat Microsoft. Have 500,000 customers worldwide (on long-term contracts. Have $5 billion in annual revenue.

2 SWEET SPOT

Who are your selected customers?

Small, medium and large businesses, who wish to automate their sales, marketing and other functions, and are early adopters of software as a service.

5 CHANNELS

How will you get your product to market?

Strong direct sales model supported by internet marketing and industry partners. Free 30 day trials, followed by sales calls to close. Sales driven culture with aggressive customer acquisition.

3 MEASURABLE VALUE

Where is your measurable value?

Deliver low cost, low risk and fast results for customers. Make solution deliverable to the business user with as little IT involvement as possible.

4 BEAT THE COMPETITION

Why should customers choose you rather than your competitors?

Reduce the time for customers to adopt new innovations through a partner developer community who deepen Salesforce's offerings. Enhance customer intimacy even though we are acquiring customers fast. Focus on the sales business buyer.

At the beginning of this book, we gave you a promise that we would get your strategy down on one page and show you how to execute it.

Your Battlecard is your one-page strategy and basecamps are the key to execution. If you've followed the process this far, you should be in a much better place to grow your company than when you began.

You now have a template for strategy creation, which you can run through every time you face a tough decision or new opportunity. The more you run through the process, the easier it becomes.

The steady rotation of the virtuous circle is the sound of a strategy working.

Take your **Business Battlecard**, lock it away, and share it only with your team. A general who broadcasts his strategy doesn't win too many battles. Surprise your customers, wrong-foot your competitors and keep your partners on their toes. Remember what Sun Tsu said about his enemies:

'They may see my tactics, but they'll never understand my strategy.'

GLOSSARY

Acquisition See Sales Cycle phase – Acquisition

Adoption Curve See Market Lifecycle

Basecamps A mountaineering term, used to describe the 'checkpoints' where your team comes together to review and test progress with the Business Battlecard, recalculate the risks, and prepare for the next phase of strategy implementation.

Buying Influencers The six individual buyer roles that may me involved when a company makes a purchase, and whom you have to convince of your value (see also **Line of business manager, User, Evaluator, Financial buyer, Procurement buyer** and **Internal champion**)

Channel Any route that helps you get your product to customers. Channels can be **direct** (in-house sales force), **indirect** (partners, resellers, distributors), or the **internet**.

Company Activities We divide all company activities into four main areas – Customer, Product, People, Finance. **Customer** refers to all customer-facing activities, and is the responsibility of sales and marketing and customer support; **Product** is your product, offering, solution, or professional service (such as consulting) and is the responsibility of Product Management and Engineering; **People** is your staff and skills capability and is the responsibility of the leadership team and HR; **Finance** is accounts, shareholders and investors and is the responsibility of the CEO and CFO.

Conservatives /Sceptics Buyers who wait until a product is fully established before purchasing at the **mature phase** of the **market lifecycle**. They often wait until everyone has jumped on board and the product is commoditised.

Customer See **Company Activities – Customer**

Customer Intimacy Customer intimate companies embark on a journey with each customer, anticipate needs and share rewards.

Distinctive Competencies Those areas – should be no more than two or three – in which your company excels. Your distinctive competencies answer the question: what are you really good at? Examples include world-class design, branding, or skilled staff. They should always convert into superior value for the customer.

Early Adopters	Buyers who value innovation and are prepared to take risks by investing in new products
Evaluator	The person in the buyer's organisation who is concerned with how well your product fits with in-house products, standards and expertise. The evaluator has a bias against bought-in products.
Finance	See **Company Activities – Finance**
Financial Buyer	The person in the buyer's organisation who is concerned with the cost of the purchase, as well as its impact on revenue, cost reduction or return on investment.
Growth Phase	See **Market Lifecycle – Growth**
Introductory Phase	See **Market Lifecycle – Introductory**
Industry Expert	The person, often a veteran, who knows all there is to know about your sector and what your competitors are doing. Companies should cultivate industry experts who will be willing to give objective advice.
Industry Segment	The sector in which you specialise and where you should be seeking prospective buyers. You should have a strong background in the segment and an understanding of competitors' strengths and strategies.
Internal Champion	The person inside the buyer organisation who really rates your product and will communicate your value in your absence.
Legal Buyer	See **Procurement buyer**
Line of Business Manager	The person in the buyer organisation who has functional responsibility for an area of business and control over a pre-approved budget. Frequently the CEO or general manager and often your main contact during a sales process.
Market Lifecycle	The stage of development of the market. Also referred to as the adoption curve. There are three main stages: the **introductory phase** is when new products are introduced and early adopters buy; the **growth phase** is when **pragmatists** decide the product is worthwhile

and often put downward pressure on prices; the mature phase is when even the **conservatives** and **sceptics** start buying and the product becomes commoditised.

Mature Phase	See **Market Lifecycle – Mature**
Measurable Value	The tangible value that the customer receives from a product. Answers and backs up the question: how much does this product make or save the user?
Mindset	Your company's core way of thinking and acting. Answers the question: how do we do things round here? Mindset is a combination of ambition and core values and is relatively unchanging over time. Examples of mindset include: 'Customer is king' or 'Cut costs' or 'Be innovative'.
Off Strategy Customers	Customers who don't fit into your defined target, don't have a critical need for your product, and don't appreciate your **distinctive competencies**. Such customers hinder growth by forcing you to put resources into areas where you have limited competence.
Operational Excellence	Companies which pursue operational excellence tend towards standardized operations and procedures and apply continuous downward pressure on prices. Think Ryanair and franchise businesses.
People	See **Company Activities – People**
Post-sales Support	See **Sales Cycle – Post-sales support**
Pragmatists	Price-conscious but savvy buyers who don't take risks but recognise when a product has proved itself. They tend to buy at the growth stage of the **market lifecycle**.
Procurement Buyer	The person in the buyer's organisation who finalises the terms and conditions of a deal, negotiates water-tight contracts and looks for price concessions. Also called **Legal buyer**.
Product	See **Company Activities – Product**
Product Leaders	Those companies which excel at innovative product development and create a buzz around their launches. Think Apple and Sony.
Proposal	See **Sales Cycle – Proposal**

ROLE	Acronym standing for **R**educe, **O**mit (or Outsource), **L**eave, **E**nhance. ROLE is a modifier for refining company activities. Companies should ROLE through activities in order to hone, streamline and improve. Valuable activities should be enhanced, and wasteful and inefficient activities reduced or omitted.
Sales Cycle	The phases of the sales process. There are five main phases: **Lead-generation** is when initial contact is made with prospective customers, often through the internet; **Qualification** is when the seller assesses the likelihood of the customer buying. Information gaps and potential risks are identified and addressed by sales teams. Qualification is continuous throughout the sales process. **Proposal** is when the seller positions his product as the winning one and gives evidence that he can deliver on promises; **Acquisition/Close** is when the customer is about to sign a contract and risk and price are uppermost in his mind; **Post-sale** is when the customer is anxious to see the product implemented and delivering benefits.
Shared Vision	The deep purpose which expresses your company's reason for existence, defines its direction and provides inspiration for the whole team. Your shared vision answers question like: What are we going to build? What will success look like? What are we going to be famous for?
Stretch Objectives	Concrete goals in areas such as revenue, customers, staff and product types or offerings. They include specific timescales for completion, but are ambitious, stretching the team beyond what they believe today.
Sweet Spot	'Sweet spot' is a golf term alluding to the favoured spot on the clubface, where contact with the ball feels best. We use it to describe the favoured spot where your product meets its ideal customer. 'Sweet Spot customers' are the ideal or on-strategy customers you should concentrate on.
Tendency to Adopt	The tendency of a customer towards buying at the **introductory**, **growth** or **mature phase** of the **market lifecycle**.
User	Person in the buyer's organisation concerned with the day-to-day operational issues of using your product.
Virtuous Circle	The opposite to a vicious circle. When your strategy is working and all the wheels and cogs of your company are turning in tandem, you're in a virtuous circle and are moving forward.

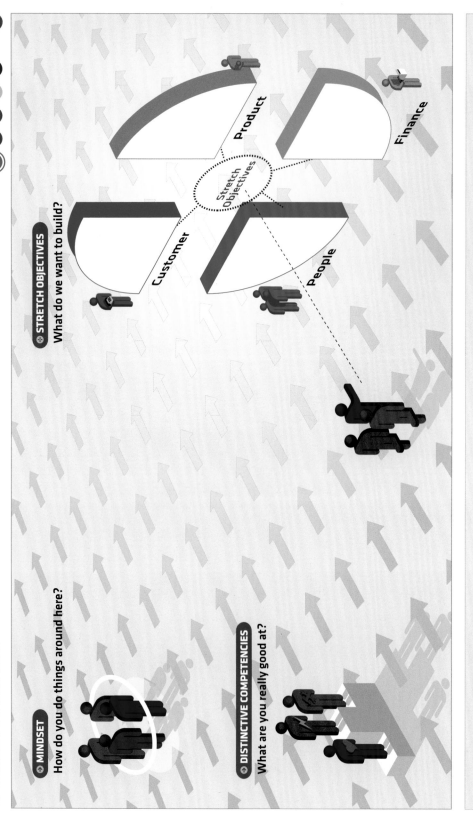

STRETCH OBJECTIVES
What do we want to build?

Product

Finance

Customer

People

Stretch Objectives

MINDSET
How do you do things around here?

DISTINCTIVE COMPETENCIES
What are you really good at?

Shared Vision Statement

↗ Sweet Spot Tool

PROFILERS · **IDEAL** · **OFF-STRATEGY**

Industry Segment

Tendency to Adopt

Business Discipline

Budget

Key Decision-Maker

Key Customer Need

Sweet Spot Statement

Create Measurable Value Tool

WHO WE NEED TO CONVINCE

TITLE

BUYING INFLUENCERS

Line of Business Manager

The User

The Evaluator

The Financial Role

The Procurement Buyer

The Internal Champion

PAIN

MEASURABLE VALUE

Measurable Value Statement

↘ **Beat The Competition Tool**

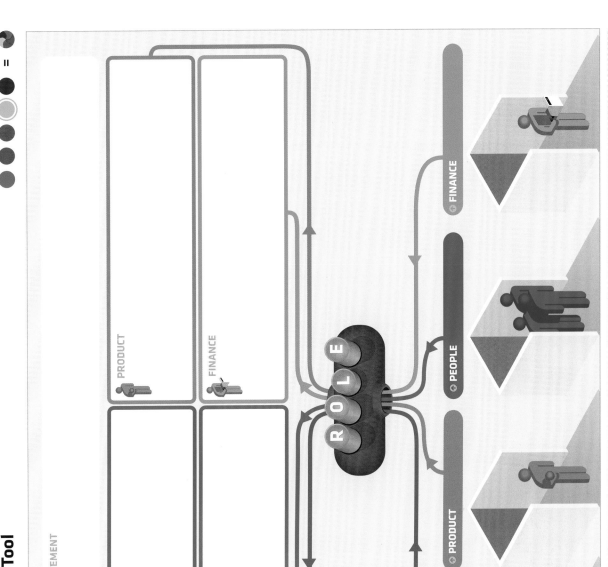

⊙ BEAT THE COMPETITION STATEMENT

CUSTOMER

PEOPLE

PRODUCT

FINANCE

R O L E

MODIFIER

⊕ CUSTOMER

⊕ PRODUCT

⊕ PEOPLE

⊕ FINANCE

Modifier options

R Reduce

O Omit or Outsource

L Leave

E Enhance

Channel Code Tool

SALES OBJECTIVE	DIRECT	INDIRECT	INTERNET
Lead Generation			
Qualification			
Proposal			
Acquisition/Close			
Support			

Channel Code Statement

Business Battlecard™
Winning moves for growing companies

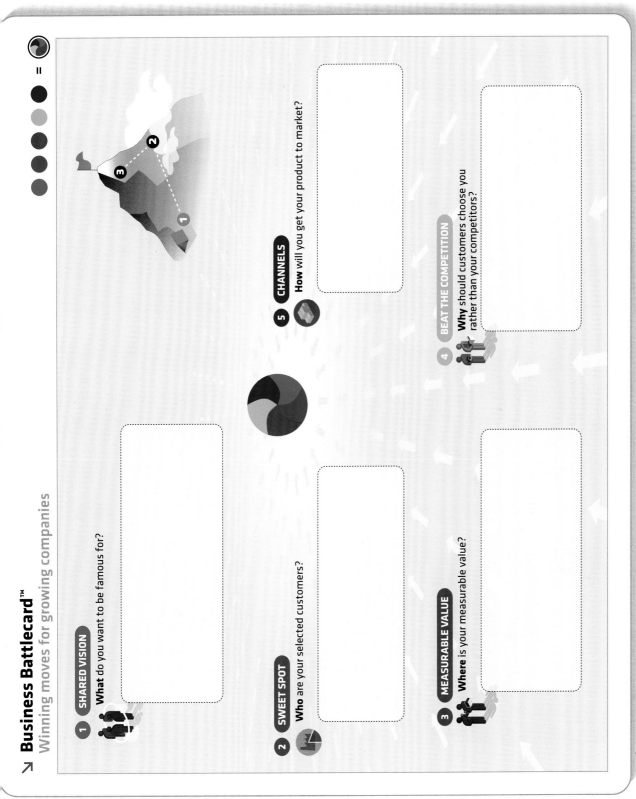

1 SHARED VISION
What do you want to be famous for?

2 SWEET SPOT
Who are your selected customers?

3 MEASURABLE VALUE
Where is your measurable value?

5 CHANNELS
How will you get your product to market?

4 BEAT THE COMPETITION
Why should customers choose you rather than your competitors?

Paul O'Dea is CEO **Select Strategies**, a strategy consulting practice, which helps leadership teams make growth happen. Clients include Expedia, Hewlett Packard and numerous investor backed companies. An engineer by profession, Paul has co-founded and helped build several companies, particularly in the technology sector. He serves on the boards of a number of growth companies, and is co-author of a previous book, *Select Selling*.